T E A C H E R
Renewal

Stories of Inspiration to Balance Your Life

T E A C H E R
Renewal
Stories of Inspiration to Balance Your Life

DALE L. BRUBAKER
LARRY D. COBLE

ON TRACK PRESS, INC. • CLEMMONS, NORTH CAROLINA

On Track Press, Inc.
PO Box 157 · Clemmons, North Carolina 27012
Phone: (336) 712-3396
www.schoolleadershipservices.com

Cover and book designed by KCL Creative - www.kclcreative.com

Printed in the United States of America

ISBN: 0-9760355-9-6

FOREWORD

This is a must-read for every teacher! It is easy to read, thought-provoking, and inspirational. It is arranged so that the busy teacher can read and contemplate one article each week. When a teacher is discouraged, it will create hope. It will encourage teachers to make a positive difference in the lives of students and to recognize and appreciate the influence they have.

As a former teacher, principal, and Director of Professional Induction and Success for beginning teachers and principals, I see many wonderful opportunities for reading and discussion of this book as a group endeavor. Teachers can create a "book club" of sorts, where they meet once a week to discuss the article for that week. This would build trust, close relationships with peers, professional development, and better understanding of colleagues and students. The teacher's world is often one of isolation, and it is important that teachers get together for fun, fellowship, and growth.

In many schools, veteran teachers provide sessions for support of beginning teachers. Articles in this book should be used as a part of the agenda for each meeting. Every new teacher needs to learn "the power of a smile" and the "value of relationships," as well as numerous other lessons from this book. It is hoped that teacher leaders will start such sessions where none are offered.

The principal who is working to create a "learning community" in the school would be wise to purchase this book for each teacher, and to use it at every staff meeting. Discussion of questions and use of activities at the end of each article would turn meetings into times of interaction and fellowship. Teachers would learn to develop passion and use it to make their teaching more creative. The principal could use these articles to promote positive attitudes among staff members.

The authors of this book are teachers of passion, who know the importance of "not going it alone." They have the gift of inspiring and motivating others. They recognize the strengths in each student and encourage students to share knowledge gained from their daily lives as a part of classroom learning. Every educator can benefit from the stories of Dale Brubaker and Larry Coble!

Doris Henderson
Guilford County School System
Greensboro, North Carolina

PREFACE

*"The great teachers fill you up with hope and shower you
with a thousand reasons to embrace all aspects of life."*

Pat Conroy *(2002, p. 63)*

An educator's life is difficult and challenging. To recognize this is to take the first step in creating a meaningful vocation. There is an important difference between having a job and experiencing a sense of calling. Teachers, as well as other educators, share a present-day reality that influences everything they do. They live in a culture of *extreme busyness*. In fact, a new term, *multi-tasking*, was created to describe this reality. When you step outside of the teacher's work world, you enter the larger society that is also a beehive of activity. We have discovered in working with teachers and other school and school-system leaders that there is little time to read extensively in order to enrich their personal and professional lives.

Teacher Renewal: Stories of Inspiration to Balance Your Life was written in order to afford you, the teacher, windows of opportunity to read brief inspirational stories that can make a difference in your personal and professional life. Why have we titled the book as we have? *Renewal* is often a wake-up call, a profound rebirth of energy as you move toward an important purpose or cause. Without such energy, you are simply going through the motions of teaching and leading, something that has little meaning for all concerned. With directed energy, your vocation and life have clarity, meaning and vitality, a gift to others and yourself. Your resources in general and energy in particular must be guided toward an encompassing and worthy goal. The way this goal is framed and expressed varies from teacher to teacher.

The subtitle of our book, "Stories of Inspiration to Balance Your Life," was chosen because of our strong belief that positive messages to teachers are more helpful than negative ones in trying to live a more balanced life. There is a real difference between being told "You're not good enough" and inspiring you to teach better and live a more satisfying life. Negative messages that assign blame and shame don't inspire teachers. In fact, they have the opposite effect. By contrast, "gifts or talents required by the language of praise" can be cultivated in an authentic way and in the process the person using such language will reinforce the understanding that "belief in oneself is necessary to all human achievement" (Conroy, 2002, pp. 156 & 398).

Most of the essays in this book celebrate the good news that teachers have found ways to live a balanced life. Some stories will leave you with the feeling that the teachers described are living lives that are *somewhat* out-of-balance: "How can I give enough attention to my teaching and my family?" "How can I help students with special challenges while at the same time giving enough attention to students who are doing well and need my resources?" "How can I balance my professional life with my personal life?" Occasionally, a teacher will share a story about a life that is or has been *seriously* out-of-balance. It is our view that all persons experience brokenness in some way at some time in their lives. It is during these times that it is natural to feel that one's life is seriously out-of-balance. The challenge is to be inspired to turn breakdowns into breakthroughs, and this depends on a support system that helps heal the heart and mind. As with any healing, however, pain and hard work test our physical and spiritual selves. It is easier to live a life in which we pretend that we're not broken. There is a gift, however, in working through brokenness: For the rest of your life there will be a moment of recognition between you and others who experience a similar brokenness (Yankoski, 2005, p. 216). Creative teachers know this and understand that where there is creation there is life. You will find this theme in the stories that follow.

Most of us have been through times when we needed to heal from medical and spiritual crises. The Kennedy family went through this when twelve-year old Ted Kennedy Jr. had to have part of his leg amputated due to cancer, followed by painful treatments. Boston Celtic coach Red Auerbach and star player John Havlicek walked into Kennedy's hospital room with a signed basketball from the team and spent three hours with him. His treatments were scheduled around Celtics games on Sunday afternoons as something to look forward to. Senator Ted Kennedy remarked: "I've learned having been on the Health Care Committee for many years in the Senate, how children mend in the midst of a medical crisis depends a lot on their attitude and on their disposition. If their minds are set and there is a sense of inspiration and happiness, they have a much better chance to recover" (Auerbach & Feinstein, 2004, p. 264). We think of this story in writing about teachers who experience healing and renewal.

There is a reading in this book for each of the 40 weeks of the typical school year as well as a reading for each of the 12 weeks during the summer. We invite you, however, to tailor the readings to any time and program sequence that fits your needs. For example, some educators tell us that they keep the book on a bed stand, kitchen table, work desk or other easily accessible place to read whenever they have a chance. Others are members of book clubs, some of which meet before or after school for brief periods of time. Still others indicate that the essays are valuable in preservice and inservice settings, such as seminars and retreats. School and school-system leaders often join teacher leaders in participating in these activities.

The essays may be viewed as snapshots-brief sketches or narratives-that illustrate key points in a personal way. The effect of these snapshots is to take you, the reader, backstage into the lives of teachers. At the end of each reading, there are questions to stimulate personal reflection and/or group discussion. There is also space at the end of each reading for you to record your answers to these questions.

As noted in our previous books, we have read the professional autobiographies and journals of more than 300 teacher leaders and other school and central-office leaders who have been in our seminars. We have drawn upon this data and our own experiences to describe the twists and turns that teachers take in the seasons of their careers and lives. Some narratives are composites.

Resources constitute the final section of the book. They may be read and reacted to privately or in a group setting. Staff development leaders tell us that the resources are an important instructional and learning aid in seminars and workshops. *References to appropriate resources will be made throughout the readings for easy identification.*

An important question may be asked at this point: *What is the relationship between the readings in this book on teacher renewal and what is realistically needed in order to make schools more effective?* Linda Darling-Hammond, a foremost scholar on schools and schooling, speaks to this question in a provocative article titled "A Marshall Plan for Teaching: What It Will Really Take to Leave No Child Behind" (January 10, 2007, pp. 48 & 28). She argues for five incentives that would in a matter of a few years lead to a first-rate teaching force in all communities:

1. "First, the federal government should establish *service scholarships* to cover training costs in high-quality programs at the undergraduate and graduate levels for young and midcareer recruits who will teach in high need fields or locations for at least four years."

2. "Second, *recruitment* incentives are needed to attract and retain expert, experienced teachers in high-need schools."

3. "Third, as is true in medicine, the Marshall Plan for Teaching should support improved preparation."

4. "Fourth providing mentoring for all beginning teachers would reduce attrition and increase competence."

5. "Finally, preparation and mentoring can be strengthened if they are guided by a high-quality teacher-performance assessment that measures actual teaching skill." (Italics hers)

In pilot testing the fifty two readings in this teacher renewal book and discussing the results of their efforts, seminar participants found a correlation between each reading and one or more of Professor Darling-Hammond's incentives.

In conclusion, the following readings and resources are designed to serve as a springboard that will inspire teachers and others to teach and lead more effectively. We invite you to enter into conversations with us by writing to us at the following e-mail addresses: dlbrubak@uncg.edu and lrrycble@bellsouth.net. We promise a response.

ABOUT THE AUTHORS

Dale L. Brubaker is Professor Emeritus of Educational Leadership and Cultural Studies at the University of North Carolina at Greensboro. He also served on the faculties of the University of California at Santa Barbara and the University of Wisconsin at Milwaukee. He received his doctorate in social foundations of education from Michigan State University. He is the author or co-author of numerous books on education and educational leadership, including *Creative Curriculum Leadership* (1994, 2004), *The Hidden Leader: Leadership Lessons on the Potential Within* (2005, coauthored with Larry D. Coble), *The Charismatic Leader: The Presentation of Self and the Creation of Educational Settings* (2006) and *Staying on Track: An Educational leader's Guide to Preventing Derailment and Ensuring Personal and Organizational Success* (1997, 2007, coauthored with Larry D. Coble). He was a teacher in Michigan public schools.

Larry D. Coble is Managing Associate with School Leadership Services, a division of The Coble Professional Group, a leadership and management consulting organization, and Director of the Collegium for the Advancement of Schools at the University of North Carolina at Greensboro. He provides speeches and seminars on leadership nationwide. He was a Senior Program Associate at the Center for Creative Leadership and served as teacher, assistant principal, principal, and superintendent in school systems in North Carolina. He received his doctorate in educational administration from the University of North Carolina at Greensboro and is author of *Lessons Learned From Experience: A Practical Developmental Source Book for Educational Leaders* (2005), coauthor of *The Hidden Leader: Leadership Lessons on the Potential Within* (2005, with Dale L. Brubaker) and coauthor of *Staying on Track: An Educational Leader's Guide to Preventing Derailment and Ensuring Personal and Organizational Success* (1997, 2007, with Dale L. Brubaker).

CONTENTS

Starting
A NEW SCHOOL YEAR

Anticipation is a wonderful and awesome mix of thoughts and feelings. Teachers, parents and students hope for the best, while at the same time being somewhat nervous about the new school year. After all, we have had plenty of experience as children and adults with regard to schools and schooling. We want to continue the good times and not repeat the bad ones.

One of the things that was missing from our teacher education programs was an understanding that teachers have different attitudes and expertise with regard to starting, maintaining and completing projects. Some teachers love and are good at start ups; others enjoy and are at their best in the maintenance mode; and some teachers like being excellent closers. Recognizing and appreciating these different attitudes and levels of expertise provide the rationale for teams and teaming. Teachers with differences can cover for and learn from each other. It is sometimes helpful to think of start ups, maintenance and closure as we do the three seasons of the school year: fall, winter and spring. "Each season has a corresponding job" (Kidder, 1999, p. 162).

Jerrika, a middle school teacher, describes her love for start ups: "I vividly remember how much I enjoyed tennis, swimming, dance, soccer and other sports. Some of my friends took lessons and were very deliberate about these sports, but I simply jumped in and used any natural talent I had. I was the same way in playing board games and things like croquet. I figured that I could learn the rules as I went along, usually from my friends who were stuck on the rules. I was like this with teaching. I couldn't wait to get in front of the students and teach. Student teaching bored me until I could have the feeling that I was the teacher in charge. Fortunately, the teacher with whom I did my student teaching appreciated my being proactive and let me begin teaching at the beginning of my student teaching. She understood that start-ups energized me." Some of Jerrika's friends, who were more deliberate in their approach to teaching and learning, also enjoyed start-ups. They loved preparing the way for the school year. They saw the planning process as a time when they could get their ducks in order. Jerrika said to a colleague on her teaching team, "You have all your ducks in order-even the dead ones."

There are also teachers who are at their best in the role of the maintaining mode. Carl, a member of Jerrika's teaching team, was like this. "I have problems in getting started but once I am on my way, I'm fine. The tortoise won the race, not the hare. Some teachers are quick off the starting blocks, but they quickly lose interest and can't be counted on after that. When we do committee work, especially accreditation reports and things like that, I volunteer for assignments. Principals and assistant principals appreciate the good work I do on these committees. My students also like the fact that they know what I expect of them. There is consistency in my classroom, and students know where I stand."

Bill calls himself "THE CLOSER" and is proud of his ability to finish tasks. He uses sports metaphors to describe his role. "When I was involved in sports, I always loved close games. I wanted the ball in basketball when the score was close, especially at the end of the game. Some of the guys on the team didn't feel this way, and so I was one of the few players who moved toward the ball when the game was tight. I was the same way in baseball. When the score was tied at the end of the game, I wanted to be up to the plate to make the difference. I was willing to risk striking out or making an 'out' some other way. I loved the rush I got in these situations. I feel the same way about teaching. There is something about finishing an assignment or even the school year that gives me the feeling that we have been successful."

The challenge to each of us as teachers is to be honest with ourselves and others as to our interests and talents. We can then decide what resources we want to use in order to improve our teaching to help students *and* ourselves. Understanding oneself is both a joy and hard work. Pat Conroy (2002) says this best: "I cheered as I retreated to the country place I keep behind my eyes, the place I return to in times of danger and despair, the hermitage and refuge I kept secret to all but myself. I was the only one with the key to this inn of interior peace that I had built on the other side of retinas and corneas and the soft tissues of my face. It is the place I go to every day to write the books which explain who I am to myself" (p. 163).

Please use the blank space that follows in order to take notes on your perceived interests and talents with regard to start ups, the maintenance mode and finishing. Give attention to those talents and interests you celebrate as well as those that you wish to improve. Share these notes with colleagues on your teaching team and invite them to participate in a conversation about these matters. [See Resources D, E and F.]

PROFESSIONAL DEVELOPMENT CAN MAKE A
Difference

It was a crisp fall day when teachers returned for the year. My colleagues (from kindergarten through high school) and I had already prepared our classrooms and we met in the high school gymnasium where our superintendent of schools welcomed us. As a first-year teacher, I had no idea of what awaited us at this meeting. The superintendent talked to us about the importance of professional development and made clear his view that each classroom was a microcosm or miniature community that represented our country and indeed the world. He then introduced a professor of international education from Teachers College, Columbia University. I was fascinated by this professor's speech. He was charismatic and well informed about how technological and cultural changes are shrinking the world, the result being that our classrooms would have tremendous teaching and learning opportunities not available to us in the past. His speech was given as if he had prepared it just for me. I heard from someone during my undergraduate years that a professor is a textbook wired for sound, but not this professor. I vowed then and there to share the guest speaker's ideas with my students, and it was during this speech that I seriously decided to consider becoming a professor someday. This was a defining moment in my life.

As I reflect on what happened to me at this particular time in my career, I realize how professional development experiences can be perceived in different ways by different teachers. I'm not sure how my colleagues reacted to this speaker, but I am sure that he planted seeds for my career and life that he never saw bloom. I am reminded that many teachers, myself included, sow seeds that we never see flourish.

Please use the blank space that follows to describe professional development experiences that have spoken to you in a positive way, perhaps somewhat like that described in the previous essay. How do you explain their value to you at the particular time you experienced them? In other words, how did the experience meet your needs and interests at the time? [See Resource G on professional development.]

PRACTICAL
Compassion

Herbert, a senior at Albion College, a liberal arts college in Michigan, briskly walked across the campus on a cold, wind-swept day in February. Raised in a small town, a pocket of poverty largely inhabited by German immigrants, he had little money and no top coat. Midway across the campus quadrangle, Samuel Harrison, President of Albion College, stopped Herbert and asked him why he wasn't wearing a coat. Herbert responded by saying that he simply didn't have one. Dr. Harrison took off his coat and gave it to Herbert as a gift. Herbert protested, "But you won't have a coat then," to which Harrison replied, "Don't worry, I have another one in my closet at home."

Herbert told this story throughout his life and said it was a turning point in his life. He finished undergraduate school and went on for his master's degree at Northwestern University, the only one in a family of twelve children to graduate from college. As with many first-generation college graduates, he opened the door to higher education for his three children, of whom I (Dale Brubaker) am one, and his nine grandchildren. My guess is that many of you are first-generation college graduates who have made a similar difference in the lives of those you love. This is what we have heard from a number of educators in our seminars. There is a sense of pride in their faces as they share their stories.

President Harrison demonstrated *practical compassion*, the term that Karen Armstrong uses in a moving book titled *The Spiral Staircase* (2004) to describe acts of loving kindness that place others, rather than self, at the center of life. As Tracy Kidder (1999) says in *Home Town*, "A place can't function or improve through compassion alone, but it can't become a good place without it" (p. 210). A classroom or a school is such a place.

Please use the following blank space to describe acts of practical compassion that you have experienced in educational settings and life itself. Also describe acts of practical compassion you have initiated along with how you felt when participating in such acts. [See Resources A & B.]

Passion

We live in a time when people, including our students and colleagues, are easily discouraged. It is, therefore, our challenge as teachers to uncover possibilities and bring them to their attention. Our passion for what we love is the key to meeting this challenge.

Turn to any dictionary to find a working definition of passion and you will find that it is a strong fondness and enthusiasm of a powerful and compelling nature. How does passion come to play in teaching? Arthur M. Schlesinger, Jr. (2000), adviser to President Kennedy and author of *A Life in the Twentieth Century,* described passion as "the marvelous quality of intensifying life so that others feel that they have perceived more and thought more and understood more" (p. 282). Our guess is that those teachers who influenced you the most in a positive way had this quality.

Passion can help you as a teacher to set aside or work through fears and anxieties associated with what you are doing, and in the process, help you gain confidence. You are so immersed in what you love that the somewhat awkward feelings we sometimes have in teaching are simply beside the point.

Passion can focus your attention so that you aren't distracted by less important matters. It must be consistent, persistent, and disciplined in order to avoid fickleness and faddism. The passionate leader is often a "nudger" who keeps others and self on track. Passion doesn't always have to be dramatic and highly visible.

Because passion is driven by curiosity, it often leads to new discoveries and keeps your ego in check. The teacher who is a good listener and conversationalist communicates love for the task at hand in order to realize organizational and personal vision. Clock watching simply doesn't exist. Top-down hierarchies designed to control people are beside the point, and ownership, not imitation, is the norm.

Teachers who feel a passion for their work often turn the mundane into something more. Simple kindnesses-notes, phone calls, e-mail messages and comments of concern about difficulties that others experience-become significant when others receive them.

Passion is pivotal for the teacher. It's a necessary condition for creative teaching. The important role that passion can play makes it clear that creative leadership is much more than a list of technical skills. Attitudes and understanding are at the heart of meeting the leadership challenge in any aspect of life, not just teaching. And the driving force for such attitudes and understandings is one's passion. (Brubaker & Coble, 2005, pp. 90-91)

Please use the following blank space to write notes on your reactions to this essay. What role has passion played in your teaching? How did the passion or lack of passion on the part of your teachers influence you and the way you teach? What ways have you found to stimulate passion in your teaching? Please give examples where possible. [See Resources A & B.]

DOING WHAT YOU *Love* TO DO

Doris knew from the time she was a child that she wanted to be a teacher. She would sometimes take her friends to the nearby school playground after school and on Saturdays to play school. She was, of course, the teacher while playing school. When Doris became a teacher after graduating from college, her pet peeve was when teacher friends at parties were asked what they did and some would say, "I'm just a teacher." For Doris, teaching was a calling, not simply a job, and it deserved respect from the public in general and educators in particular.

Unlike Doris, Jim entered the teaching profession after working for a bank in Atlanta for five years. He had been at the top of his professional development classes at the bank and was placed in charge of the division that granted loans to prominent corporations at the end of his fourth year at the bank. He had just reached a salary bracket that placed him in six figures. Although he had no teacher education classes during his undergraduate years, he had taught Sunday school classes during his high school and college years and thoroughly enjoyed the experience. Drawing on his strong math background at the university and years at the bank, Jim decided to enter a lateral entry program to become a high school teacher in the city's school system. Jim came to life with his teaching and professional development experiences designed to help him catch up with teachers who had strong preservice education programs in universities. He no longer felt that he was on automatic pilot, as he was at the bank. He looked forward to work each day and felt connected with teaching, learning, students and colleagues.

Jim and Doris started their teaching careers at different times in their lives, but they share the joy of doing what they love to do-a gift to others and themselves. They will face difficulties in their careers and lives as they grow older, but they will be bolstered by a passion for their vocation that money can't buy. Veteran singer and songwriter David Crosby describes the rich dividends passion for one's vocation plays in his book titled *Since Then: How I Survived Everything and Lived to Tell About It.* When asked what it was like to have turned 65, he replied: "I have a lot of things wrong with me, and so there are a lot of medical problems and stuff. That makes it harder, but you don't know that when you're playing. As soon as you start playing, all that goes away" (Sachs, 2006).

How will you know when you experience the joy of doing what you love? You will find yourself losing track of time and you won't have to worry about the twin enemies of boredom and depression. You will be totally connected with the creative process and those engaged in this process with you. Frank McCourt (2005), author of the best-selling book, *Teacher Man* said it best: "Find what you love and do it" (p. 255).

We were interested in finding out how students know that their teachers care and want to be with them. A few of their responses are powerful. Mitch, a fourth-grader, said, "My teacher came to see me play tennis after school." Ellie, his sister, responded: "My sixth-grade teacher brought a bunny to class to teach us responsibility-to feed it, clean its cage and give it attention." Georgia, a twelfth-grade student in a government class said, "My teacher held special seminars in his home with authors of paperbacks we read as guests. He and his wife also hosted non-juried art shows in their home where we could show our art work." These teachers believed that *curriculum is life,* not simply a textbook.

Please use the following blank space to describe those times when you experience what David Crosby talks about. What are some of the ways you can help yourself and others have such experiences? [See Resources A & B.]

Reaching
EMERSON

When Emerson walked into my ninth grade classroom, everyone knew it. He was outspoken and not afraid to share his thoughts and feelings. In fact, he reminded me of a famous speaker who visited our large metropolitan church, a man who dominated the pulpit with his bearing and speaking skills. He, like Emerson, presented himself in such a way that you knew he had to be reckoned with, whether or not you wished to do so. On that first day in meeting Emerson, I thought he would be a formidable member of a high school debating team. He was articulate and loved to present ideas that provoked discussion.

One of the first things that Emerson said to the class was that he got his clothes from the Salvation Army because his parents couldn't afford store-bought clothes. This comment, of course, called attention to the clothes he was wearing-a patchwork of items that were not coordinated. He then informed us that he slept on the floor in his home as there was no mattress or bed for him. He didn't come across as bragging or complaining about his family's poverty. Rather, this was simply the way things were in his life.

As with any classroom, students get into a routine after a few days and size up each other as they form relationships. It was at this point that Emerson's outspokenness, particularly with regard to ideas on the edge or over it, became a problem. Students shut down and simply no longer listened to Emerson. He was isolated by his peers. Some even enjoyed excluding Emerson. As Tracy Kidder (1999) reminds us through one of the characters in his book, *Home Town*: "At the right distance, injustice looks thrilling" (p. 205). Another character adds: "Hey, we're getting along great today! It's just miserable stuff we deal with. And it's fun. It's not happening to me" (p. 150).

I knew how easy it would be for a teacher to pile on and therefore further isolate Emerson. Most of the students in this ninth grade class were compliant and took fewer teacher resources than Emerson. I found Emerson's ideas, off-the-wall as some of them were, stimulating and worth considering in our class discussions. I knew I had my work cut out for me. When Emerson said things that were important to the topic at hand, I would repeat or paraphrase what he said and then call on students by name to ask for a response to the idea. Emerson was pleased that his ideas were being considered, and the students in the class recognized that I would not join them in discounting Emerson.

Emerson taught me a lot about teaching and the importance of including, rather then excluding the dissonant voice. Frank McCourt (2005) speaks to this matter in an insightful and humorous way in his book titled *Teacher Man*. "The great American drama is the clash of adolescence with middle age. My hormones beg for a quiet clearing in the woods, theirs are brassy, throbbing, demanding" (p. 254). He adds, "Find what you love and do it. That's what it boils down to. They may like you, they may even love you, but they are young and it is the business of the young to push the old off the planet" (p. 255). Emerson helped me see that teaching was what I loved. McCourt concludes: "The classroom is a place of high drama. You'll never know what you've done to, or for, the hundreds coming and going. You see them leaving the classroom: dreamy, flat, sneering, admiring, smiling, puzzled. After a few years you develop antennae. You can tell when you've reached them or alienated them. It's chemistry. It's psychology. It's animal instinct. Find what you love and do it" (p. 255).

Please use the blank space that follows to describe how you have been challenged to reach students isolated by their peers in the classroom. Also, note how you have used activities outside the classroom to reach these students. Finally, what are your views on the comments made by Frank McCourt? [See Resources A & B.]

Listening

A number of teachers and their spouses, all of whom were new to the community, started an informal group that met on Saturday nights for dinner and conversation in our homes. We enjoyed each other's company and established a kind of trust and good will that newcomers often share. As you might guess, the men gathered in the kitchen after dinner to talk about sports while the women sat in the living room talking about things other than sports. All the men went to the kitchen except for George who stayed in the living room with the women. He was accepted, respected and well liked by the women. No problem! One night after one of our evenings with the group, I asked my wife: "What is the story with George? Why does he always sit with the women in the living room, and why do you all like him so much?" She responded: "You don't get it, do you? George is a good listener." I got the message. Unlike George, the rest of us men at the dinners were not good listeners.

Listening is probably the most powerful civility available to people in general and teachers in particular. It is flattering to the speaker, and it demonstrates that you aren't self-centered, but instead are eager to learn more about the person speaking. By focusing on the speaker, you will also lessen your anxiety. By actively listening, you will communicate that you understand where the speaker is coming from and care enough about that person to step into his or her shoes.

Make no mistake about it. Listening is hard work, what M. Scott Peck has called a manifestation of love (Peck, 1978). It relies on the discipline of bracketing, "the temporary giving up or setting aside of one's own prejudices, frames of reference, and desires" (Peck, 1978, p. 128). The true listener temporarily communicates total acceptance of the speaker, the result being that the person speaking will feel less threatened and make himself or herself more vulnerable by telling you more.

One of the most important things I learned as a teacher about the power of listening is that colleagues and students don't usually want an answer to the problem that they bring to my attention. They simply want someone to listen attentively to their venting. Once I realized that there was no need for me to try to fix their problem, a good deal of pressure was taken off of my back, and they went on their way feeling better. It was difficult for me as a teacher to come to this understanding since I had inadvertently fallen into a trap associated with being a helping teacher who wanted to fix, heal and take away the pain. I wanted to take them across the street rather than letting them go there by themselves.

Please use the following blank space to note your reactions to this essay? What is your view of your own listening skills? How have you learned about the power of listening? What steps do you still need to take to be a better listener? Are the teachers that you know good listeners? Why or why not? [See Resources D & E.]

Enthusiastic
COMPETENCE

It was a cold December night as we made our way along two-lane rural roads to Ellie's middle school for the holiday orchestra concert. Nearly a hundred students were to perform in sixth, seventh and eighth grade orchestras. The tip off that this was going to be a special evening was Ellie's bright-eyed, energetic invitation. She said that she wanted us to hear her orchestra and meet her orchestra teacher. Her enthusiasm made it clear that she wanted us to be there, *and* she wanted to be there.

Dr. Stewart, the school's principal, introduced Ms. Barefoot and conveyed his pride in the school's music program; the PTA president led us in the pledge of allegiance; and the seventh grade orchestra played the national anthem. Ms. Barefoot's presentation was self-assured and articulate and let the audience know that she had high but realizable expectations and standards for her students. The faces and body language of the students in the three orchestras told us that they took what they were doing seriously, while at the same time they were being creative and enjoyed themselves. The orchestra director's leadership was obviously a model for her students.

Ms. Barefoot and the students invited Mr. Hawkins, a physical education teacher, to read holiday stories that introduced different selections played by the orchestras. His resonant voice was applauded by the audience, and Ms. Barefoot gave him a present from the orchestras. What better example of teacher teaming and cooperation could we have had! Ms. Barefoot previously had a competition for stories written by students, and the winner beamed as her story was read.

Discipline was not an issue as members of the orchestra immersed themselves in their performances. They were as well behaved in listening to the other two orchestras as they were with their own performance. Ms. Barefoot had prepared the way with practice sessions. How different the self-discipline of the students was in contrast to another school's music program. The director, while standing in front of the stage, thumped the palm of her right hand on the stage to keep the students in line during their performance. Needless to say, this interrupted the flow of the program.

As we left the school, one parent summed up our feelings about the evening: "What a difference good teacher leadership makes in a school!" Ms. Barefoot must certainly have felt pride in her students and her work, but she had little time to think about such matters as she was focused on the holiday band concert she would direct the following night.

Kahlil Gibran (1923) wrote in *The Prophet*: "And if you sing though as angels, and love not the singing, you muffle man's ears to the voices of the day and the voices of the night" (p. 28). On this night, they played as angels and loved the playing, for which the audience gave thanks.

Please use the following blank space to describe performances like the one in this essay that you have experienced. What difference did teacher leadership make in such performances? What ideas and feelings have you had when you provided such leadership? Please give specific examples to illustrate these ideas and feelings. [See Resource F.]

Seeing CLEARLY

It was my last semester as an undergraduate, and it was time to review lecture notes in order to take the final exam in the World Religions class. It was during this semester that I also had courses in literature, drama and history. To this day, I can vividly recall studying at my small desk in a rented room in a large Victorian house. While sitting there, I began connecting insights from the lecture notes in World Religions to ideas from literature, drama and history. Facts and concepts, parts of a puzzle, came together in a larger framework of knowledge. I constructed the larger picture in my mind's eye.

The next morning I entered the World Religions' classroom with a quiet confidence I had not experienced previously. I felt like I was on the wings of angels in writing answers to the essay questions before me. I had integrated learnings from my four courses in a personally satisfying way. What I didn't realize was that I was in the middle of a "perfect storm", one created by questioning the prevailing wisdom of a professor who segmented knowledge for his own instructional purposes.

The following day I received a phone call from the professor. He asked me to come to his office to discuss the exam. Although he was affable, it was obvious that he was troubled by what I had written. He simply said, "I only wanted you to write about what you had learned in my class." I left his office with an exam grade of C+, what the professor believed was an acceptable compromise between my creative essay and his expectations.

Although I didn't realize it at the time, this experience was a turning point or marker event in my life. I made a commitment that I would integrate knowledge when I became a teacher. And so it came to be that my social studies students would be invited to weave insights from learnings, wherever they occurred in their lives, into our classes together. We defined curriculum as life, and in the process, inspired each other to learn more and share more with each other. What we did was to question the traditional view that students are simply empty vessels to be filled with the teacher's knowledge base.

Charles Kimball (2002) speaks to what we had learned: "Of all the senses, sight is the one most closely connected with knowledge. When someone 'sees' something, she or he 'knows' in a powerful way. Someone who understands something deeply has great 'insight.' We commonly revere people who have a 'vision' for the future or whose 'foresight' is proven to be accurate" (p. 96). What a joy it is as a teacher when students see clearly, often by questioning prevailing wisdom and create their own knowledge frameworks.

Please use the following blank space to record those times when you, as a teacher or educational leader, have experienced clear vision by questioning prevailing wisdom and creating your own knowledge frameworks. How did others respond to your new insight(s)? How have you encouraged your students to question prevailing wisdom? To create their own knowledge frameworks? What were the joys and challenges in doing this? [See Resource H.]

HOW OTHERS CAN HELP US SEE
Clearly

Although each of us ultimately makes the decision to do this or that, others can play an important role in helping us see clearly and therefore make better decisions. Our vested interests or lack of knowledge often create blind spots that can only be identified by others. It takes an act of courage, if not desperation, to reach out to others to ask for their help. Our fears often kick in at such times, as we know that we are making ourselves vulnerable to what others might say. But, once we experience the benefits of help from others, we can continue to seek insights with greater assurance and confidence. This depends on the awareness, even appreciation, for what we don't know. Alvin and Heidi Toffler (2006) speak to this matter: "Today so much knowledge is needed for good decision-making that the smartest people know what they don't know" (p. 125).

As a beginning teacher, I had little understanding of school politics. My most recent models for being a teacher were provided by university professors, and I didn't understand the very real differences between university culture and school culture. Some of the bureaucratic norms or "rules of the game" in school, such as sending absence and tardy slips to the principal's office, struck me as mundane paperwork, and I simply didn't follow them. When I shared what I was doing with a friend-a veteran teacher-she quickly informed me that the secretary ran the school, and I had better stay on the secretary's good side, or I would be in a lot of trouble. I quickly discovered that I was already in a lot of trouble.

But it was with regard to the matter of what constituted the best content and instructional approaches to such content that my colleagues were most helpful. Once my colleagues checked me out and found that my questions in meetings were authentic, from the heart and head, I realized how important a learning community can be. It became clear to me that there were many instructional approaches, and as professional teachers it was both our responsibility and joy to be able to clearly articulate what we were doing and why. It was in going through this process that I learned to improve my teaching and learning.

Parker Palmer (1999) discusses the role a "Clearness Committee" of five or six trusted persons can play. Focus is on asking honest, open questions rather than fixing. "The process can become a way to renew community in our individualistic times, a way to free people from their isolation without threatening their integrity, a way to counteract the excesses of technique in caring, a way to create space for the spirit to move among us with healing and with power" (p. 48).

Please use the space that follows to describe ways in which others have helped you see your blind spots. In what ways have you helped others who have invited you to identify their blind spots? Please use concrete examples to answer these questions. [See Resource F.]

THE POWER OF A
Smile

It was an early Saturday morning in November when I woke up exhausted after nine weeks of teaching, with three long weeks until the Thanksgiving break. I slowly moved around the house with little motivation for doing anything-especially anything connected with school and teaching. I wondered what it would be like to simply go back to bed and wake up just in time to begin teaching on Monday morning. I knew that I wasn't seriously depressed, but I also recognized the signs of feeling lower than I wanted to be.

As lunch time neared, I had little interest in eating anything, and yet I knew I needed to get something in my stomach. Even the thought of walking two blocks to the small restaurant near my home seemed like a huge task. I then remembered what I did in high school when I felt the way I did today: I went to a café where friends hung out, ate French fries and a cheeseburger, drank a coke and listened to music. The thought motivated me to walk two blocks to the hole-in-the-wall restaurant near my house.

I approached the order window that separated the eating area from the kitchen and experienced a smile and greeting from the woman taking orders that I will never forget. Without thinking too much about it, I noticed that my spirits picked up immediately. I then reflected on how my daughter in her early teens would bring friends home, and they often had what I called "winning smiles" on their faces. I knew when I saw these smiles that these kids would make it in the world they faced in the future. No matter what jobs and careers they had, they knew how to greet the public.

A staff development workshop I attended when school started in the fall had a speaker who advised us to be at the door of our classrooms to greet students when they walked in each morning. The speaker said that such a greeting would let the students know that their teachers wanted to be with them. She added that when she visited some classrooms a few students with low self concepts appeared to crawl along the walls to avoid teachers when entering their classrooms.

How powerful can a smile be? After 76 days adrift when his sailboat capsized in the Atlantic Ocean, Steven Callahan was given a gift on shore. "I unwrap the gift and behold a great prize: a mound of chipped coconut cemented together with raw brown sugar and capped with a dot of red sugar. Red! Even simple colors take on a miraculous significance.

My smile-God, it's so strange to smile-feels wrapped right around my head" (Callahan, 1986, p. 311). Mike Yankoski (2005) endured similar hardships for several months as a homeless person in a few cities in the United States. What really mattered to Mike and his friend, Sam, as they weighed how others treated them? "I think the most meaningful gift might be your genuine attention and caring. It was amazing how much a smile or quick hello did for Sam and me on the streets, partly because such kindnesses were so rare. When someone stopped to talk, even for a minute, the powerful underlying message was, 'I notice you, you're a human being, and you're worth my time'" (p. 174).

Please use the blank space that follows to describe an experience you've had when a person's smile lifted your spirits. Also describe how your greeting with a smile was received in a positive way by another person or persons. What ways can you name to let students know that you want to be with them in your classroom and school? [See Resources D, E and G.]

NOT GOING IT ALONE –

Learning

TO VALUE RELATIONSHIPS

In writing her professional autobiography, Susan, a veteran teacher in a small high school, said that she had lived a solitary lifestyle as far back as she could remember. Her older sister left home for the university before Susan entered high school. Susan recalled an adolescence where she put dinner on a TV tray and headed for her bedroom to spend evenings away from her parents. It wasn't that she felt animosity toward her parents. She simply felt that they had their lives, and she had hers.

Susan was an honor student throughout high school and college. She channeled her perfectionist tendencies toward established goals and met them with distinction. Her "Lone Ranger" attitude and behavior weren't openly challenged until she took a professional development leadership seminar as a first-year department chair.

It was a shock to Susan when she was criticized by fellow department chairs during a simulated decision-making activity. Team leadership was called for, but Susan openly held back, saying that she had found that she could perform tasks in her school more efficiently by herself. She stated that shared leadership was simply another fad that let poor performing and unmotivated people waste their time, as well as her time as a department chair. She added that she knew that her candid views on this matter were not popular but they were accurate.

The consultant leading the seminar had experienced reactions like Susan's before, and knew that backing Susan into a corner would not help her see a position other than her own. The consultant, therefore, hit the pause button in the simulated activity and went to the flip chart stand in front of the room. She said that the group would brainstorm reasons for and against shared decision-making. This was done in an even-handed way, so that there were clearly advantages and disadvantages on the flip charts. Seminar participants then returned to the simulated decision-making activity for the remainder of the session.

Susan learned from this seminar experience but still had a good deal of work to do in reconciling her desire for autonomy with the need for collaboration. Susan's charmed life reached an impasse during her third year as a department chair. Working harder and longer in order to solve problems in her department and family fatigued her to such an extent that she sought professional help. She was advised that medication would help her cope with the difficulties she faced, but in the long run, she would need to make important changes in order to turn a "breakdown" into a "breakthrough." With time, hard psychological work and practice, Susan began to understand that suffering is an essential part of the change process and connecting with others is an accommodation that helped her curb her inclination to always control persons and settings. Parker Palmer (2002) writes: "Our schools, colleges, and professional development programs can and should teach much more than they do about the tragic dimension of life-about the fact that no amount of intelligence and goodwill can wall us off from events that threaten to crush us; about the fact that such events, rightly appropriated, can enlarge our lives; about the fact that forgiving and letting go play a critical role in transcending our condition" (p. 313). Palmer (2002) adds: "Good teachers suffer because they wear their hearts on their sleeves-but they learn how to suffer creatively, turning pain into self-knowledge, personal growth, and professional service" (p. 312).

Susan learned that she still needed solitude, a time to look within, but she also needed time with others. At the end of her professional autobiography, Susan celebrated the joy she finally began to experience in embracing her new understandings and leadership. She also received a bonus she didn't expect. She now had empathy and understanding for teachers and others who experienced "breakdowns."

Please use the space that follows to describe how you relate to Susan's narrative. Can you identify with it? Have you observed others who have struggled with Susan's challenges? How have you and others reconciled such matters? How can you help those you lead concerning such matters? [See Resources F, G and H.]

Commitment

The difference between saying something and doing something is highlighted in the following sayings: "Talk is cheap!" "I hear you talking, but what is the reality?" "Walk the talk!" "It's easy to say, but let's see you do it!" A teacher, concerned about health issues, approached the manager of an exercise center, who offered a group membership if 10 teachers in the school would sign up at a discounted price. The teacher leader introduced the idea at a faculty meeting, and there was a good deal of enthusiasm. Over twenty teachers signed a paper circulated around the room indicating their interest. Heartened by this appearance of commitment, the teacher leader distributed membership forms a few days later. At the end of the month, only three teachers submitted completed forms and submitted a check to the teacher leader. She wondered aloud, "What happened?"

Roland Nelson, formerly at the Center for Creative Leadership in Greensboro, North Carolina, has constructed a Commitment Scale/Hierarchy that helps leaders honestly assess what they and those they lead are willing to do on behalf of a particular commitment to an issue:

1. I will sacrifice my life and/or the lives of my family and/or those I dearly love.

2. I will give up the respect of those whom I love and I'll forego my status and professional achievement.

3. I will forego economic security and my career.

4. I will have serious conflicts between what I think should be done and my reluctance to do it. I may alter my work style and give up those techniques that had previously been successful and beneficial and learn new ones.

5. I will have to alter some habits with which I'm quite comfortable, thus making my job somewhat more difficult. I will feel uncomfortable from time to time as I do things in a way that don't seem, based on my past experience and present assumptions, to be best.

6. Past experience indicates that it doesn't make any difference between Tweedledee and Tweedledum (Brubaker & Coble, 2007, pp. 88-89).

We have found it useful to place a copy of this commitment scale in prominent places where we can refer to it when we are involved in decision-making situations: on a desk, in the front of an appointment book, and in a notebook we take to meetings. We frequently distribute the scale to colleagues and others in professional development settings and discuss how it can be useful to teacher leaders.

Being honest with yourself and others about your commitments takes courage, "the most precious asset anyone can bring to the public arena" (Califano, 2004, p. 491). Courage is the bedrock of two other characteristics necessary for success in the public arena: determining the right course of action, and having "the tenacity to stay the course" (Califano, 2004, p. 492).

Please use the following blank space to record your reactions to this essay. What experiences have you had as a teacher with regard to the rhetoric-action distinction? How might you use the commitment scale in teacher leader situations and other leadership contexts outside of the school? [See Resource C.]

Determination

Lloyd DuVall, a prominent educational and governmental leader, learned as a child to combine musical talent and self-discipline. This is another way of saying that he learned the value of determination. He began playing the piano in the second grade. With encouragement from his musical family, he soon performed "concertettes" for other classes in his school.

DuVall knew at the age of 8 that he wanted to play in the Ohio State University band, one of the finest marching bands in the nation. But, in his own words, "I was a terrible trumpet player." Fortunately, a new high school band director arrived a few years later and suggested that he switch to the tuba. In his junior year of high school, he won first place in state competition for playing a Bach violin sonata on the tuba. In his senior year, he auditioned for and gained entry to the Ohio State University School of Music.

DuVall's self-management skills integrated musicianship and athletic ability in the marching band at Ohio State University. He carried a 30-pound Sousaphone, swung his left arm, marched at 180 steps per minute, lifted each leg parallel to the ground on every step, and played music memorized for that week's performance. As a sophomore, he was named manager of the band.

As manager, he recognized the importance of personal satisfaction and group harmony. He learned that the leader creates the conditions for organizational effectiveness by communicating objectives and ways to reach them. DuVall was awarded the honor of being the dot in the i when the band spelled out Ohio State on the football field.

DuVall used his determination to achieve success. He could have dropped out of high school band when he had difficulties playing the trumpet, but with the help of an equally determined teacher, the band director, he switched to the tuba. He also recognized the need for balancing individual effort with teamwork: "I am intrigued by the role of personal pride in the organization and its influence on the quality of organizational performance. I remember the price band members paid at Ohio State for making serious mistakes during a Saturday performance. They were treated to an unceremonious dunking in the Olentangy River on Monday and would be forced to wear a sandwich board painted in the colors of archrival University of Michigan at every practice during the week. These standards were set and enforced by band members, not the director."

DuVall is an example of the firmness of purpose or determination that one must have to be a successful teacher. A teacher has to be willing to try new ways when old ones fail and in the process be candid about what hasn't worked and why. Self-pity and a sense of being victimized on the part of a teacher who makes mistakes is counterproductive and works against one's positive sense of self and teamwork. (Brubaker & Coble, 2005, pp. 135-137).

Please use the blank space that follows to note reactions to this essay. What role has determination played in your getting to the place you are now as a teacher? How did you deal with difficulties along the way that could have led to your not becoming a teacher? Give concrete examples where possible. How has a lack of determination worked against you and others at particular times? Please describe how this problem has caused some teachers you have known to leave teaching. [See Resource F.]

Courage

Courage is one of the most fascinating and elusive subjects a person can study. It takes many forms and depends to a large extent on the context in which it is practiced. For example, a teacher assistant in an elementary school was the only person who stood up to the principal in a faculty meeting when the principal wanted to assign parking spaces based on a person's position in the hierarchy. For example, the principal got the best space, followed by teachers, after which teacher assistants, cafeteria workers and custodians were assigned their positions in the parking lot. The school culture had a history of such practices, even to the extent that teacher assistants knew they were not to cut birthday cakes at birthday parties for teachers. The state legislature passed legislation that placed a teacher assistant in every kindergarten through third grade classroom in order to improve reading instruction, and principals were not paid more for providing supervision of these newly assigned teacher assistants. Some principals resisted this new legislation, saying that they wanted more teachers, smaller classes and no teacher assistants.

What qualities did this outspoken teacher assistant have that caused her to successfully challenge the principal so that parking spaces were not assigned, but instead acquired on a first come, first served basis? First, she felt that any criticism of her stand on the parking space issue was criticism of a downtrodden group of employees in the school. Second, she had a history of being an articulate spokesperson for any group in the school that she felt was treated unfairly by the principal or anyone else in the school system. She had experienced success in the school, school system and community. Third, she was respected by many of those with whom she worked, excluding the principal, for her sense of justice and her willingness to act on her beliefs. Fourth, her "reward was inward clarity, and the price perpetual anger or, at best, discomfort with the world, not always on the surface but always there" (Kidder, 2003, p. 210). She felt most alive with her passion refreshed when she stood up for what she thought was right. She had a kind of moral indignation that she referred to as "divine discontent." She was willing to take the heat when she followed her moral compass. (Brubaker & Coble, 2005, pp. 173-190).

Barbara Ehrenreich (2005) writes about the plight of the white-collar unemployed in *Bait and Switch:* "What they need, too, is not a 'winning attitude' but a deeper and more ancient quality, one that I never once heard mentioned in my search, and that is courage: the courage to come together and work for change, even in the face of extreme difficulty." This is evidenced in another one of her books titled *Nickel and Dimed.*

Please use the following blank space to take notes on your critique of this teacher assistant's leadership. How would you relate to her if she were your colleague? In what ways was the context, the culture of the school, a factor in her success? If you were a teacher or teacher assistant in this school, what would you have done in response to the principal's assignment of parking spaces and why?

Curiosity

Moving from Lansing, Michigan to Santa Barbara, California opened our family's eyes to a new way of life. Southern California was like living in a supermarket that never closed. Driving our car westward through state after state exposed us to scenery vastly different from what we had experienced in the Midwest. During our four years in California, we were alive with the curiosity that comes with exploring a setting and culture in sharp contrast to our origins. From there we went to Milwaukee, Wisconsin for two years, after which we moved to Greensboro, North Carolina, a mid-point between the Appalachian Mountains and the Atlantic Ocean. Our first visit to Oriental, North Carolina, a small seacoast community, once again made us feel as if we were visitors from Outer Space. We got out of the car and walked toward a long table where a number of young people with black aprons were standing. One of our children, full of curiosity, asked them what they were doing. "Heading shrimp," one of the workers replied. Rube that I was, I turned to my wife and said, "I didn't know shrimp had heads." Our children continued to ask a number of questions that the workers answered while continuing to work at full speed. Finally, one of them suggested that we go to the nearby shrimp boat to talk to Captain Jim about shrimping. We did, and found him helpful and patient in answering our questions about where and how shrimp are caught.

I frequently think of this story in reminding myself that curiosity is the fuel that drives learning wherever it takes place-inside of schools and outside of schools. It is why it is so much fun and also sometimes tiring to be around curious little children. They are full of awe, wonder and amazement as they explore the world around them. Adults are frequently in such a hurry that we don't even see things that children stop to stare at and touch, such as caterpillars and bugs on the ground. Their curiosity immerses them in the joy of learning so that time and place take a backseat to the excitement of the moment. And, this joy is contagious. Simply consider the things that grandparents do with their grandchildren, many of which they would not do without their grandchildren present: swimming, digging holes in the sand at the beach, flying kites and riding bikes.

We are challenged as teachers to create settings and environments that stimulate the qualities of exploration and learning that we experienced as children turned on to the world around us. I sometimes introduce something I am teaching by saying, "I want to be sure that at least one person today is turned on to learning, and I would like to nominate myself as that person, because then I believe you will want to be curious and learn as much as I do."

The leader in the classroom, like the leader in the school, sets the tone for how learning takes place. This is an awesome responsibility and opportunity that must be taken seriously. Show me the teacher who is motivated by learning, and I will show you a learning setting that is alive. Show me the teacher who is not, and I will show you a setting where there is little, if any, life.

We are wise to remind ourselves of the awe, wonder and amazement we had as children when we were driven by curiosity. Robert MacNeil (2003), a Canadian who is among the most respected and admired journalists of our time, did this in writing *Looking For My Country: Finding Myself in America:* "I felt a richness of emotion in childhood memories that would surprise no psychologist, and I realized that those feelings had informed the experiences I'd been having in all the other places. Memory is not just about the past; it continues to inform and alter the present" (pp. 161-162).

Please use the following blank space to take notes on how curiosity played a significant role in your learning in and outside of school. What do you do when you don't feel this curiosity as a teacher and learner? What ways have you found to stimulate curiosity when you feel it is missing? Please give examples to support your answers.

DECOMPRESSING FROM THE

Holidays

Another out-of-town family holiday is over, and I will return to my teaching tomorrow. There seems to be a predictable cycle to these holidays. Step one is the anticipation of time off from work and preparation for the trip-travel plans, what we will eat and what we will do when we are together. Step two is our warm greetings when we see each other again. Step three is when we settle in for the vacation, doing this and that and having long conversations when there is spare time from physical activities. Conversation time is when we push each other's hot buttons on issues like religion, money and politics. On occasion, differences lead to meltdowns-those times when those who choose to enter the battle empty themselves of their raw feelings about matters anchored in past events, usually from childhood: "You never took me seriously!" "You always thought you were smarter than I was!" "You never listened to what I had to say!" It is during this time when one or more in the family will threaten to pack up and leave, head for their bedrooms or simply pout. Step four is the remainder of the vacation. Hard feelings may linger or family members may simply go about their business feeling better for releasing their feelings. It goes without saying that each family member comes to the four stages in his or her own particular way acting out feelings about conflict and community.

All of this is exhausting, of course, and that is why it will be good to go to work again on Monday. We can get in our routines with people who probably haven't experienced us in our childhoods and family situations. We can share what happened over the holidays with those we wish to talk to, and some troublesome things we experienced may actually be quite humorous as we tell our stories.

I talked to a good friend at work after he returned home from a holiday at the old home place with seven brothers and sisters. He said that they all pitched in to paint the house. I said: "Oh, that must have been wonderful being together again!" He responded: "It was terrible. We all returned to our old roles and relationships with each other. It was miserable!" I reminded myself of how we tend to project our images of what a vacation should be on others, and such projections don't necessarily reflect what really happens.

M. Scott Peck (1987) has created a useful framework with four stages of community: (1) pseudocommnity, (2) chaos, (3) emptiness, and (4) true community. *Pseudocommunity* is the stage when members of the group come together and generalizations and platitudes about things held in common prevail. Hugs and exaggerated civilities are the order of the day. *Chaos,* the second stage, occurs when individual differences emerge. Peck. (1987) believes that "chaos always centers around well-intentioned but misguided attempts to heal and convert" (p. 90). Some within the group want things to be *normal* as different individuals fight to control the agenda. The sheer noisiness of this stage, chaos, leads many to invoke control. Some attempt to define the rules of engagement during this stage. *Emptiness* is the third stage, the most difficult stage in creating community, and yet it is "the bridge between chaos and community" (Peck, 1987, p. 95). Persons "need to empty themselves of barriers to communication" (p. 95). Personal prejudices and priorities come to play during this stage. *True community* is a rare mix of time and place. The group decides, often without saying too much about it, where to go from there. Peck (1987) cautions us not to think that life in true community is easier or more comfortable: "But it is certainly more lively, more intense. The agony is actually greater, but so is the joy" (p. 105). When you experience true community, you simply know it.

The lessons we learn about creating community in our families can be invaluable in creating community in our educational settings and vice versa. Sensitive educational leaders have an eye out for such learnings and apply them in their lives in general and work settings in particular.

Please use the blank space that follows to describe how you have used what you have learned about creating community in families in your work place and vice versa. Share any examples from family vacations in your description. Can you identify with persons in this essay? [See Resources F & H.]

Hope

Mrs. Birch, the director of food services, was nearing retirement. She was a "mother" to all who knew her, thanks to her generous spirit and kindness. She is a person worth listening to, and so we paid special attention to the story she was telling: "All of you know that I've been a member of a small rural church. Have been for years. We have a new, young minister fresh out of seminary at Duke, He's something! He has long hair, he dresses informally, and you won't believe it, but he now has a processional and recessional, even though our church choir only has eight people in it. He doesn't stand behind the pulpit but instead, walks right out into the congregation to give his sermon. And you should see his wife! She dresses like a hippie. She has this long, stringy hair, says pretty much what she thinks, and doesn't care who hears it. She could care less about serving at teas in the parsonage like our other ministers' wives did, and she has all of these New Age posters that she painted displayed on the church walls. I'll tell you, they are something! You know why I like them? They are optimistic and that's exactly what this aging congregation needs!"

Those of us listening to Mrs. Birch were surprised at the punch line. It was obvious from her final comment that what we took for major issues were minor in Birch's mind, because the minister and his wife would bring life and a hopeful tone to a church that needed it.

In thinking about those teachers who made a positive difference in our lives, we came to the conclusion that they all had a heightened sense of curiosity, a passion for their work and the ability to leave us with the hopeful feeling that we could make a difference in creating a better world. They sent a message to us that the power of one and the power of people working together mattered.

Their commitment to teaching and others was a kind of love that is not afraid to feel the pain experienced by others and themselves. Instead of sidestepping pain, they let themselves feel it head on, and in making themselves vulnerable, those of us who were their students shared more of our feelings and ideas. We connected with each other, rather than distancing ourselves from each other.

The realistic but hopeful teacher knows that this understanding and behavior can't be forced on others, but can be a living example that others may or may not choose to follow. It is counterproductive to "sermonize" profusely or try to back insensitive others into a corner, but by "walking the talk," each of us can make a positive difference in our own lives and perhaps the lives of others. (Brubaker & Coble, 2005, pp. 103-105).

Please use the blank space that follows to take notes on the role that hope has played in your teaching and life. How have you responded to teachers who are hopeful? To those who are not? How have you maintained hopeful attitudes and behavior when those around you are not hopeful?

Teaching

AN OCCUPATIONAL HAZARD

Things happen to a teacher every day that speak to what good teaching and learning are and conversely what poor teaching is and how it works against productive learning. Our desire to teach is an occupational hazard, one our own children and others remind us of when they find it annoying. Preachers' children warn their parents not to preach, and teachers' children tell us to stop teaching! As teachers we can't help it. We are always looking for lessons to be learned in our experiences.

For example, our family went to a favorite restaurant to celebrate our daughter's birthday. We were greeted cordially by the hostess and led to our table. The waitperson approached our table and said, "Can I help you?" in a voice devoid of emotion. She wasn't unpleasant, and she wasn't pleasant. She was simply there. Our family reacted to her flattened affect by trying to pick up her spirits with humor and caring comments. No response. The result of this lack of interaction with the waitperson-the leader who was expected to set the stage for a pleasant evening-was that the food was excellent but the total dining experience was not. As a teacher, I had to make sense out of this experience *and teach my family members what I learned*: "Can you imagine this! What kind of teacher would our waitperson make!" One of our children said, "Give it a rest, dad. You're not in your classroom now." It was obvious from the looks on other family members' faces that they supported my antagonist.

On another occasion, I took one of our children to a six-bay lube station to have oil in the car changed. It was mid-morning when we arrived, and I was surprised to see that none of the bays were filled. I asked the receptionist when my car would be serviced and she said, "I'm sorry but no one showed up for work this morning. It's a real problem these days, isn't it?" At this point I turned to my child and said, "Can you imagine what would happen to me if I didn't show up to teach?" I then went on and on talking about how important it is to be dependable. I was interrupted in my lesson by my child who said, "Why don't we just go down the street to another place to have our oil changed?"

I smile in telling these stories about my teacher behavior because I know that all working persons experience occupational hazards, and there isn't a whole lot we can do about this. It is natural that our work settings give us frameworks from which we speak and act. It is part of teaching lore that as teachers we have "that teacher look"-the ability to stop people in their tracks by staring at them. So be it. It comes with the territory.

Frank McCourt (2005), in his wonderfully humorous book, *Teacher Man*, argues that a teacher's authenticity is a key to success: "You can fool some of the kids some of the time, but they know when you're wearing the mask, and you know they know. They force you into truth. If you contradict yourself they'll call out, Hey, that's not what you said last week. You face years of experience and their collective truth, and if you insist on hiding behind the teacher mask you lose them. Even if they lie to themselves and the world they look for honesty in the teacher" (p. 203).

Please use the following blank space to take notes on your reactions to this essay. Do people outside your school catch you and tell you that you sound like a teacher? How do you react when this happens? Do you find that others you know have a certain look or sound associated with their professions? Elaborate. Do you want to do anything about your answers and if so, what is it that you want to do?

THE ROADS WE DON'T INTEND TO
Travel

A teacher nearing retirement was asked about the most important thing she learned during her career. Her response reflected a kind of wisdom that only comes with rich and varied experience: *"Some things work out for the best even though it doesn't feel like it along the way."* When asked for examples, she told the story of her career choices: "I had a business administration major in college, something that led me into real estate sales after graduation. I threw myself into this work and made myself available for every opportunity. After five years, I reached a six figure salary. I had everything the family I grew up in never had-a luxury car, a large house in the suburbs and recognition as a success in business. But something was missing, and I didn't know what it was. It was at this time that the bottom fell out of the economy in general and the real estate business in particular."

She continued, "A friend of mine in high school, who graduated from the same university I did, had become a teacher. Then she returned to the university for a master's degree in educational administration and was in her first year as a school principal. Knowing that I was actively involved in many of the same extra-curricular activities with her in high school, she asked if I had ever considered being a teacher. She invited me to sit in on classes taught by some of her best teachers. Fortunately, these teachers were not only excellent classroom teachers, but they also gave leadership to some of the extra-curricular activities that I especially enjoyed as a high school student-the school newspaper and the yearbook. I now had the bug, and returned to my alma mater to get my teaching credentials, using money I had saved as a business woman. With the help of my friend in a principalship, I applied for and received a teaching position in her school system. I have never worked so hard, but it is so satisfying making a positive difference in the lives of my students. I've taken a road I never intended to travel, it has not been easy, but it is where I need to be at this time in my life."

In 1983, David J. Garrow was denied tenure by the political science department at the University of North Carolina at Chapel Hill, even though he was rated a good teacher by his students, and one of his books on Martin Luther King, Jr. won a regional political science award. The chairman of the department said that Garrow's research was closer to investigative journalism than to basic scholarship. In 1987, Professor Garrow received the Pulitzer Prize in biography for his book titled *Beating the Cross: Martin Luther King, Jr. and the Southern Christian Leadership Conference*. At the time that the Pulitzer Prize in biography was awarded, Professor Garrow was an associate professor at City College of New York. The unintended road traveled by Dr. Garrow exposed the subjectivity of teacher evaluation and gives hope to all who have suffered because of such subjectivity. Some things do indeed work out for the best, even though it doesn't feel like it along the way.

Please use the following blank space to describe roads you took even though you didn't intend to take them. What were the difficulties you experienced? How did you deal with these difficulties? What did you learn from these experiences and what actions on your part emerged from these learnings? What advice would you give to others on these matters? [See Resource H.]

Friendships
AND COMPETITION

Lee is in the sunset years of his career as a teacher. He describes himself as having a kind of wisdom that he didn't have earlier in his life and career, especially with regard to the matter of friendships. This is what makes conversations with him so interesting. His story deserves to be told in his own words:

"When I was a kid I loved sports and competition. No matter what the sport was, I took great pride in the fact that I always wanted to win. Part of this must come from the fact that I had a brother two years older, and there was a large playing field behind our house in the small town where we lived. When we had any spare time we always went to the basketball court, tennis courts and baseball field, where other kids gathered for pick-up games. I did everything early in life in part because I had an older brother, and he often found me to be an intruder who got in the way of his friendships. The first time I beat him in tennis he jumped the net, pushed me to the ground and started beating up on me. He only stopped when I yelled out, 'You can't do this. You want to be a minister!' He paused with a strange look on his face and let me go."

Lee continued: "When I got in junior high school, I played basketball and tennis on school teams and became more competitive. I'll never forget going to the bulletin board in the locker room to see if my name was on the list of guys who made the team. But competition didn't stop with getting on the team. I wanted to be on the starting five in basketball and at the top of the ladder on the tennis team. The award system, particularly in high school, was intense. Who would be named captain, most valuable player, and a member of the league, regional and all-state teams? And, or course there was the strong competition in playing against other teams. College athletics were more of the same, but at a higher level."

Lee then came to the bottom line of his story: "I didn't realize until I was well into my teaching career that I carried this competitive attitude into relationships with colleagues in educational settings. There was always a certain distance I maintained with my colleagues, particularly other men, and this got in the way of my having true friendships at work and in the community where I live. Once I was honest with myself about this, I decided that it was time to give more to my friendships and let up on the competition. As a result, I started to live a more satisfying life. Now that I am in the final years of my teaching career, I have never been happier. There is no need to compete, nothing to prove. Sometimes I look hard at a person who annoys me and say to myself, 'He's just trying to find his way-just like me,' whereas in the past I would have said, 'I've got to try to change him.' I've learned that I can make changes in my own life that may or may not lead to basic changes in the lives of others. I've learned to relax and enjoy qualities in others that I admire. I seldom have 'teeter -totter' relationships with others: 'They go up, and I go down; I go up, and they go down.'"

Please use the following blank space to note your reactions to Lee's story. Is your story in relation to competition different than Lee's story? If so, how? Have you made changes in your life and career with regard to the matter of competition? How difficult has it been to make these changes, if you have made them? Describe how other teachers you have known relate to the issue of competition. [See Resource F.]

Exuberance

Mildred Hughes is a veteran fifth grade teacher in a small rural town. When she began teaching, parents weren't sure they wanted their children in her class because of her strictness. They wanted their children to have a structured classroom, but they questioned a teacher "who didn't smile until Christmas," which is the way they described Mrs. Hughes. At the same time, they knew that fifth graders, particular boys, were a real challenge who needed to toe the line. Fifth grade boys were known for the tricks they played on each other-often to get the attention of girls. Mrs. Hughes tells her colleagues that she likes teaching fifth graders because they are just a step away from middle school, the time and place where hormones get out of control.

Although Mrs. Hughes has good background knowledge in a number of areas of the curriculum, she has a special interest in science. She believes in a hands-on approach to science, something that makes it a challenge to keep the classroom clean. She has gerbils, hampsters, fish, turtles and rabbits in her room from time-to-time. Students are taught to be responsible for keeping animal habitats clean and feeding them appropriately.

It was late in the school day on a Tuesday in April that Homer Hyatt approached Mrs. Hughes' desk and asked her if he could bring his pet monkey to class the next day. Homer was a straight A student who had not exhibited any behavior problems, Mrs. Hughes thought for a moment before answering, "Yes." She then added, "He's in a cage, isn't he?" Homer answered, "Yes."

Homer arrived at school just before the bell rang on Wednesday morning, with his monkey, named Marvin, in tow. Upon Mrs. Hughes' advice, Homer placed Marvin's cage on a small corner table about ten feet behind Mrs. Hughes' desk-a place where she had to turn her head in order to see him.

Mrs. Hughes quickly took attendance and launched into her science lesson, since she always starts the day with her favorite area of the curriculum. The smiles on the boys' faces should have been an indication of what was to come. The snickers that followed were somewhat disguised at first but quickly turned into waves of laughter that nearly shook the room. Marvin was doing what Monkeys do… in a zoo or a cage in a classroom.

Mrs. Hughes turned her head to see what was going on and then quietly but deliberately picked up the cage and took Marvin to the principal's office, where Marvin remained until school closed that day. But, it was what she did after taking Marvin to the principal's office that got the students' attention. She went to the board and wrote in large letters EXUBERANCE. She asked the students what this meant. It took some prodding on Mrs. Hughes' part but the discussion that followed finally led to a definition: *an overflowing of laughter*. Mrs. Hughes concluded the discussion by saying that there are some situations in life that are really very funny, and this was one of them.

Mrs. Hughes had thought and acted "out of the box." She let the students know that she had a side to her that they didn't know she had. She managed the classroom without assigning blame and being judgmental. She knew "when to hold 'em and when to fold 'em." Mrs. Hughes modeled her humanity for her students while keeping order in the classroom.

Andy Rooney, whose books and appearances on "60 Minutes" every Sunday night have entertained us for decades, writes: "The worst thing you can say to someone is 'You have no sense of humor.' You can tell people they dress badly or that they don't know their elbow from second base, but don't tell them they have no sense of humor or they'll never forgive you. Years ago someone asked Louis Armstrong what jazz was and Louis said, 'If you have to ask, man, you'll never know' The same is true of humor" (Rooney, 1987, p. A13).

Please use the blank space that follows in order to take notes on how you have used your sense of humor to make a positive difference in your teaching and leading. How have you reacted to situations of exuberance in your teaching and leading? Please also describe how your colleagues have reacted to humorous situations, if you have heard about such times. [See Resource H.]

KEEPING ONE'S WORK IN
Perspective

"How do I keep my work as a teacher in perspective?" a teacher asked colleagues in a professional development workshop. A veteran teacher responded by telling a story about a friend who ran for secretary of state twice in a neighboring state. John actively campaigned for office by traveling to small town after small town, handing out suggestions and favors in exchange for political support. One small town mayor wanted a job for his brother, whose employment history was spotty at best. John suggested that the mayor's brother assume the position of sidewalk supervisor checking on cracks that could be especially dangerous for children on bikes and skateboards and the elderly who were prone to falls while walking.

The mayor's brother accepted the newly created position but started to annoy the mayor and town council with his detailed requests. The first week he asked for a uniform with appropriate insignia; the second week he wanted citations printed so he could issue tickets to small business owners who had installed benches and other objects that got in the way of those who wanted to use the sidewalks, and he then applied for a place on the council agenda to report his findings on a monthly basis. Council members urged the mayor to find another job for his brother, a job whose description was clearly defined so that it couldn't be expanded by its occupant.

When the veteran teacher had finished telling the story shared by his politician friend, participants in the workshop were laughing and the teacher who asked about keeping teaching in perspective said, "I get the point! Balance is the key."

Some beginning teachers become so intensely involved in reaching children that they lose perspective. When this happens, they don't sleep well and aren't as effective as they were before their work started getting out of perspective. If they are fortunate, a wise mentor can help them reach the balance they need.

Mike Yankoski (2005) interrupted his time in college to spend several months on the streets to better understand the lives of the homeless in several cities in the United States. He struggled with what he could and could not do and learned a fundamental lesson from his efforts: "We're responsible to help others toward hope...but we're not responsible for their choices" (p. 216). And, so it is with teachers who seek a balance in their personal and professional lives. As colleagues we can help them understand some of the issues facing them, but they are responsible for their choices.

Please use the blank space that follows to describe one or more situations when you and/or your teacher colleagues lost perspective. What were the signs that this was happening? What steps were taken to achieve a more balanced work style? What are some of the ways in which you can help colleagues understand issues related to balance in their work and life?

PERSPECTIVE AS

Reality

I had never been to Mobile, Alabama, and looked forward to the social studies conference there. Accommodations at the Riverview Plaza Hotel, a high-rise structure across from Mobile Bay, were first-rate and my room had a beautiful view of Cooper Riverside Park and the water. When I woke up the next morning, I looked out my hotel window and saw light fog and mist in the park. There appeared to be a man sitting on one end of a bench in the park, his fisherman's hat the most distinguishing feature as he faced the water. I put on my jogging clothes and made my way through the hotel toward the park. After crossing the street, I approached the bench and discovered the older man on the bench was a dark green statue-an excellent likeness of a fisherman.

After working out, I returned to the hotel, showered and put on my convention clothes. It was time for a good breakfast. While in the restaurant, I started a conversation with the wait-person about the statue we could both see from my window seat. With a smile on his face, he said, "I tell people stories about the fisherman-like he's lonely, his family's all gone and he just sits there all day." It was obvious to me that the wait-person had quite a sense of humor and got a kick out of telling these stories to his customers.

The next morning I returned to the same seat in the restaurant and asked a different wait-person how long the statue in the park had been there. She responded, "That's not a statue. He sits there every morning. See, he just moved." At first I thought she was kidding, but further conversation convinced me that she was not. I asked her how long she had been working there. She said that she had been there for three weeks.

What a curious experience this was! Two of us knew the man on the bench was a statue, one of us did not, and yet each of us believed his or her perception was reality. I reminded myself of the many times, particularly in emotional contexts, when a student or parent had a perception of a situation quite different from mine. I also remembered how I learned with experience that accepting this fact was *the starting point* in having a conversation with the student or parent so that we could reach some kind of agreement. When I began teaching, I simply thought that the student or parent was wrong in holding a different view. On one occasion, an angry mother came to my room at the end of a school day and vented her anger on me. I took a deep breath and listened to her. After a period of time, she apologized, saying that her husband had just lost his job that morning. One of the advantages in being an experienced teacher is that perspective and wisdom can be drawn upon.

Frank McCourt (2005), in his provocative book, *Teacher Man*, shares stories about how he learned to relate to parents and their children so that they learn to move "from FEAR to FREEDOM" (p. 253). He adds: "I don't think anyone achieves complete freedom, but what I am trying to do with you is drive fear into a corner" (p. 253). What a powerful change of perspective!

Please use the following blank space to take notes on how you learned that others' perceptions are their realities. How did this understanding influence your teaching and learning? What are some of the difficulties a teacher encounters if other persons' perceptions of reality are not recognized as a starting point in your conversations? [See Resource F.]

EACH CLASS HAS ITS OWN
Personality

Julie is at the mid-point of her teaching career. She is in a position as mentor of a beginning teacher to share what she has learned, and yet she still identifies with the fears and dreams of a person new to the profession. After a long day of teaching, she invites her mentee into her classroom for a chat. "You probably already know this but you may not have the words to describe what I am going to say to you. When I was in college, I had courses in psychology that focused on how different people's personalities are, but I never heard anyone talk about the personality of a group of students-a class. It seems so obvious that perhaps my professors simply took it for granted. Or, maybe it is because our country puts so much emphasis on the individual-pull yourself up by your own bootstraps, do your own thing-those kinds of messages. I thought that if I learned the right teaching methods, I could use them with any class to reach my objectives. I was in for a real surprise when I had a class where only a few students were good readers. Some could hardly read at all. My first reaction was that the principal had sent me the wrong students, but then I realized that they were the only students I had. I panicked at first but then used different-level reading materials on the same subject. I also learned that some classes had good leaders in them, and other classes didn't seem to have any leaders at all. In both cases, it was my challenge to develop leadership skills in students-most of whom didn't even know that they had the potential to lead. I hope this makes sense to you. I just wanted to share what I consider to be one of the most important things I learned from my students: I had to learn how to adjust to the personality of each class as well as the personalities of students in the class."

Pat Conroy, author of *The Prince of Tides* and *The Losing Season* (2002), described this best when he returned to his teacher's classroom after graduating: "Thanks for finding me when I was a boy." His teacher replied, "No, no, no, Mr. Conroy. You always get that part wrong. We found each other, Mr. Conroy. We found each other" (p. 225).

Please use the following blank space to describe your reactions to this essay in general and how you discovered with your own teaching how to relate to the personalities of classes. Describe what you learned about this matter in your teacher education classes and staff development experiences. [See Resources F & I.]

Reflection

It was one of those Monday mornings in the middle of winter when I had to de-ice the windshield and the door locks before turning the key several times until the car began to start. I could hear the snow and ice crunch under the car's tires as I made my way into the parking lot of the school. I walked into my classroom, took off my coat and sat down behind my desk in the front of the room. The light started to stream through the windows of the classroom, and I looked down at my feet. I had done it again. I had a black sock on one foot and a brown sock on the other, the kind of thing that happens when you dress in the dark in a Michigan winter.

Fortunately, I had learned from my first two years of teaching experience to arrive at school at least half an hour before the students showed up so that I had time to get organized and reflect on what I intended to do that day in general and my lesson plans in particular. What is reflection and why is it so important to the teacher? Roland Barth (2003) defines it clearly and concisely: "Reflection is nothing less than an internal dialogue with oneself. It is the process of bringing past experiences to a conscious level, analyzing them, and determining better ways to think and behave in the future" (pp. xxi-xxii). Frank McCourt's book, *Teacher Man*, is a fascinating read precisely because he shares in an honest way the internal dialogue he experienced as a high school teacher in a variety of teaching and learning situations. He writes in one of these contexts: "I tell myself, Stop. No preaching. You did that years ago with your rant on the French Revolution. If they want to say it sucks, let them. Isn't this a free country" (2005, p. 231)?

If we shared some of our internal dialogue with our students and colleagues, we would probably be at risk. It is this kind of dialogue that Frank McCourt shares with readers, bringing a smile to our faces and hearty laughter at other times. To see the humor in our classroom encounters and laugh is a wonderful relief from our desire to control the teaching and learning process. Students probably know that we care more about them because we are willing to laugh, thus making ourselves vulnerable in some sense. It is at such times that we are most alive as teachers. Mark McCormack (1984) writes: "What are you really passionate about in life, and is there any way to make a living at it" (p. 57)? It is a gift to others and ourselves when our answer to this question is *teaching*.

Reflection is such an important part of teaching that we often take it for granted. Some summer jobs that I had while in college, such as ditch digging for a construction company, call for so little reflection that we don't fully appreciate having a vocation that values and depends so much on reflection.

Please use the following blank space to take notes on the role of reflection in your life as a teacher. What ways have you found to build more reflection into your teaching? What are the barriers in your life as a teacher that work against having adequate time for reflection and what can you do about such barriers? For example, do some people who see you engaged in reflection think that you are indecisive rather than undecided? [See Resources F & J.]

THE

Fan

We sometimes feel like we no longer want to watch the news on television or read the newspaper because so much of what we see and read is depressing. But occasionally we hear or read a story that lifts our spirits and gives us new hope. Such a story came to our attention this morning in reading about Bonnie McIntosh, a young woman with spastic diplegia, a form of cerebral palsy that tightens her muscles and makes walking very painful (Rowe, 2006, p. B3). She uses a motorized scooter to get around for any distance. She has childhood memories of insensitive kids taunting her with "Hey cripple." She and her two athletic siblings loved sports, and she went to every high school football game, home and away, regardless of the weather. When she was a sophomore, members of the football team bought two dozen red roses and gave them to her at the homecoming pep rally along with a sash that read "THE FAN." After graduating from high school, Bonnie earned an associate's degree in human services technology at a community college. Since then she has worked to help persons with developmental disabilities.

During the past year and a half, Bonnie has been a cheerleader for hard-hat workers building Center City Park, a site a block away from her condominium in Greensboro, North Carolina. Her enthusiasm for the project is contagious. "She often spots something new. Another bench. Another tree. Another funky sculpture. Then, she'll 'atta-boy' her new friends and compliment them on their work in creating the park" (Rowe, 2006, p. B1). Bonnie expresses herself so vividly: "I almost cried the day they tested the fountain because it was so beautiful. Again it goes back to freedom. I can go there and experience it like everyone else. I'm not being held back" (Rowe, 2006, p. B3).

Bonnie reminds us that there is a place for everyone who loves an activity or sport and our enthusiasm for any endeavor, such as the building of a new park or the creation of educational settings and projects in our schools and classrooms, can be an inspirational message for all who experience our presence.

Bonnie found her interior voice represented in a magazine ad: ASK PEOPLE TO JUDGE ME BY MY ABILITY NOT MY DISABILITY. Pat Conroy (2002), famous author, speaks to the joy he experienced in finding this inner voice: "I realized what it was, the truest part of me, the most valiant flowering of my character, a source of pure light and water streaming out of unexplored caverns deep within me. This voice rang with authority and spoke with a blazing, resonant accuracy, with the clearness and certainty of church bells heard on bright Sundays. It riveted me with its absoluteness of vision, its breathtaking assurance" (p. 217).

Please use the following blank space to describe what happened to you in achieving the kind of assurance that Bonnie McIntosh and Pat Conroy discovered. Give examples where possible. What are some of the things you do to maintain this sense of assurance? If you wish, describe how others you know relate to this assurance issue. [See Resource H.]

NEEDING
People

Ralph Vaughn, who recently passed away, had a special gift for the drivers who passed his home. He sat on his front porch and waved to motorists: "Passers-by responded quickly. Business people, teenagers, home-makers, bus loads of school children-they honked and waved and hollered their appreciation" (Johnson, 2006, p. B1). How did this gruff-talking truck driver and ex-Marine start this ritual? Twenty one years ago he retired after having open-heart surgery, became bored with sitting in his house while recuperating and decided he needed to be in touch with people. What effect did his waving have on people? His wife describes it best: "I've had people say they were coming home from work, they had a bad day and to see Ralph wave would lift the weight somehow. You never know what a wave will do" (Johnson, 2006, B1).

Carol, a first-year-high school student, was asked by her parents how school was going after a few anxious, uncomfortable weeks. Carol's face lit up and she said: "I was at the juice machine, and Mr. Simmons, my home-room teacher, asked me how I had lost one of the twist things in my hair. I smiled and said, 'I don't know.' He said, 'You know what I'll do, I'll buy you a drink' and he put the money in the machine. I really like Mr. Simmons." Carol's parents were relieved, for they now knew that their daughter was more at home in her new school, thanks in part to one teacher's seemingly small gesture. Carol was given special attention by someone who mattered in her life.

Robert was a real character, a student I had come to know during my third year of teaching. I never knew what he would say. One day after class, he ambled up to my desk, looked me in the eye and said, "You know what I really like about you as a teacher?" "No," I replied saying to myself, "Bring it on, Robert. Say something about my teaching methods, my being prepared for class and the exciting teaching materials I bring to class." Robert surprised me, bringing a smile to my face with his response: *I really like the way you shine your shoes. Your shoes always look cool.*

Robert and Carol's comments remind me that everything that we do as teachers counts. So much of what we do is planting seeds, and we frequently don't know if and when they will bloom. It is awesome to realize that with each student we get to know comes the opportunity to create a better world. People do need people.

Please use the following space to note experiences you have had that are similar to those involving Carol and Robert. How did you react at the time? How did you learn that seeds that you planted flourished? What can you do to remind yourself of the importance of the lessons you learned from this essay? [See Resources F & H.]

FINDING

Goodness

I just arrived at my office at the university when the phone rang. Dr. William Nolan, a professor of sociology, greeted me, asked how members of my family were doing and then asked one of the strangest questions I had ever been asked as a professor: "Bill Janson is a graduate student in one of my classes. He said that you were his advisor and so I decided to call you. Can you tell me some good things about Bill and his work that would let me give him a B- rather than a C+?" I thanked Dr. Nolan for caring about Bill and listed some of Bill's fine qualities. "Thanks for your help on this matter," Professor Nolan said, and he hung up. I noted on Bill's transcript at the end of the semester that he did indeed receive a B- in Dr. Nolan's class. Bill Janson never knew about this telephone call, but I did, and I will never forget it. Professor Nolan taught me a powerful lesson about finding goodness in others and in the process served as an example of goodness in himself.

The opposite approach to students was one that I occasionally had as a secondary-school teacher. The demands of teaching and the convergence of discipline problems with other challenges sometimes made me extremely tired, and as a result, it seemed like I was looking for students to catch making mistakes. I would literally walk the halls looking for students who were doing something wrong. I had inadvertently fallen into "the critical parent trap." Whatever a student did was either wrong or not good enough. I tried to remind myself that this was my problem when I got in this frame of mind rather than the problem of those around me, but it was still a challenge to find the goodness in students, colleagues and others, rather than slipping into a judgmental mode. Instead of finding the goodness in students, I gave the impression that parents and administrators had sent me the wrong students.

Don't get me wrong. I know that there are real problems facing students, teachers and administrators. What I am referring to is the negativism that consumes one when problems crowd out possibilities. The joy of teaching becomes the drudgery of teaching.

It takes experience to deal with one's own negativism in a constructive way. James Macdonald helped me during a dark time in my teaching. He suggested that I close my eyes briefly, particularly just before ending the day, and list three good things that happened that day. I asked for an example. He replied, "It may be as simple as taking out the garbage, having a brief conversation with a student or remembering the delight a student had in learning something new." Still stuck in a victim frame of mind, I wasn't sure I could do what Jim suggested, but I tried and it became a part of my self-discipline that remains with me to this day. It works!

In April, 2005, Irving Kristol, co-founder and co-editor of *The Public Interest,* a quarterly journal of public policy, died. Charles Krauthammer (2005) described how Kristol found the goodness in others and life itself: "Kristol knows how bad things can be, but he never-never descends into despair or recrimination. When everyone else is headed for the bunkers, he keeps his head, his good will and his humor" (p. A9). Katharine Graham (1997) writes in her fine book, *Personal History,* that she loved being with her friend, Warren Buffett: "He and his style were exactly what I needed. I was learning but having fun at the same time-learning and laughing, my favorite combination" (p. 535).

Please use the blank space that follows to take notes on how you have found goodness in others and what this did for you and others. Also describe how you moved out of dark periods when you looked for people making mistakes to the exclusion of finding goodness in them. How have others found goodness in you and what were your feelings when this happened? [See Resource C.]

BULL VS. *Knowing* YOUR STUFF

What a great feeling it is to really know what you are talking about as a teacher! You have an authentic sense of confidence, and you are at ease in sharing what you know with those you teach. You don't waste resources by faking it and then covering up your fakery when students challenge what you have said.

It is part of the human condition, however, to resort to "shooting the bull" at times. We have identified two kinds of bull: (1) low class bull; and (2) high class bull. A third grade teacher was talking about national parks in our country and mispronounced, with a good deal of assurance, Yosemite National Park. She said, YOSE MIGHT NATIONAL PARK. A third grader said that he and his family had visited the park during the summer and he questioned his teacher's pronunciation by saying the name correctly. The teacher said, "I'll look this up tonight and report to you on this matter tomorrow." Tomorrow never came. Another teacher claimed a good deal of expertise on our legal system and used legal terms in an incorrect way during a parents' "walk the schedule night." A parent, who was an attorney, raised a question about what the teacher said, and the teacher pushed ahead, thus further demonstrating his incompetence on this subject. These two examples of low class bull make clear the difficulties a teacher may face when dissembling.

We also occasionally use high class bull. Some teachers develop this into an art form. One way this is done is to use an extensive vocabulary that few in a classroom or audience understand. High class bull artists know that they are not likely to be questioned or corrected since people don't even understand the words being used. Whereas the low class bull user may simply say things like "Research says that…," high class bull artists cite research studies but distort research findings to meet their own needs. They bank on the fact that most students and others will not have read the research study cited. Politicians frequently use statistics in this way when campaigning.

We talked to one high class bull artist who said that he had perfected the art of deflection in dealing with parents who questioned what he said. He would simply smoothly change the subject to one he knew something about. He told us, "This works every time." His confidence in this matter demonstrated the power of appearing to be smart. He added: "When I am questioned in a serious way, I defer to the intelligence of the person questioning me. Sucking up this way nearly always works." Red Auerbach, successful coach of the Boston Celtics, was asked by his brother, Zang, "Is there anyone in the world who sucks up to you who you don't think is a good guy?" Red paused to consider the question, "And how," he finally asked, "does that make me different than anyone else" (Auerbach & Feinstein, 2004, p. 87)?

All of us have an impostor complex to some extent. That is, we are afraid that others will discover that we really don't know what we are talking about or doing. Lady Bird Johnson spoke about this when she was asked what it was like for her to become first lady: She responded, "I feel like I've walked on stage for a part I've never rehearsed" (Graham, 1997, p. 354). Arthur M. Schlesinger, Jr. (2000), renowned Harvard historian and special assistant to President John F. Kennedy, writes:

> Although I now rather enjoyed lecturing, I never quite escaped the impostor complex, the fear that I would one day be found out. My knowledge was by some standards considerable, but it was outweighed by my awareness of my ignorance. I always saw myself skating over thin ice. The impostor complex had its value. It created a great reluctance, for example, to impose my views on students. (p. 439)

Schlesinger had the wisdom to know what he didn't know. He didn't try to pull the wool over the eyes of his students and others. It is sometimes scary to think about those classrooms where the teacher doesn't know what he doesn't know, and neither do the students. Ignorance is simply compounded. At the same time, it is absolute joy to be in a classroom where the teacher consistently demonstrates she knows her stuff and so do her students. It is helpful to me to remind myself that presenting myself authentically is like writing a first-rate memoir, "a book in which" others hear my "true voice-the best kind of book" (Graham, 1997, p. 622). And, that's no bull.

Please use the following blank space to take notes on how you feel when you really know your stuff during the teaching process. Also note what you do when you don't and how this feels. You may use this same exercise in assessing teachers you have known. [See Resource I.]

ANXIETY AND

Presentation

OF SELF

It is so natural to fear and even try to run from anxiety until we realize that anxiety is the fuel that makes our "presentation of self" engine perform. Having a manageable edge on gets the adrenaline going. Self-talk when I am anxious can be very important: "Congratulations on being fired up enough to be somewhat nervous about speaking to the school board tonight about what teachers need. It is a compliment to the board and others in the room that you care enough about what you have to say to have an edge on."

We were in a meeting of examiners charged with deciding who would get into our doctoral program at the university. One candidate was absolutely calm during the interview. In fact, he had what a professor of educational psychology called flattened affect-no sign of feelings. This professor said to the committee after the candidate left: "Something is wrong with this candidate because there was no visible sign of nervousness."

The challenge when we feel that we have an excessive amount of anxiety is to find ways we can manage it so that we can still function successfully. Warren Buffett told Katharine Graham, who overcame her fears to pilot the *Washington Post*, about a friend in a Dale Carnegie course who was challenged to manage his anxiety about public speaking: "We're not going to teach you how to keep your knees from knocking. All we're going to do is to teach you to talk while your knees knock" (Graham, 1997, p. 537).

Ideally, you feel that what you have to say or do is of such importance that you lose yourself in the process of getting your message across. A friend feared a retirement party where he was expected to give a speech after listening to comments about his career by those with whom he worked. After his speech, he turned to us and said: "I couldn't believe how confident I felt in thanking others for being there and giving what I thought were highlights of my more than thirty years of teaching. I spoke from my heart."

There are other occasions when you feel as if you are on automatic pilot. You may even get tired of hearing yourself as you have given this presentation so many times. If possible, personalize your speech so that you bring life to it. Talking to people in the audience informally before and after the presentation will relax you and may be more important to many in the audience than the speech itself.

It is probably wise to have an emergency strategy in the event that you experience what television personalities call "flop sweat." That is, you feel paralyzed and sense that you can't continue with your speech. One speaker described his emergency plan: "I simply walk toward or into the audience and ask one or more persons how they feel about the last point I made. I have done this on a couple of occasions, usually when I begin my speech absolutely calm and shortly after, get blindsided by fear-that 'deer in the headlights' feeling. Strangely enough, we entered into a conversation that relaxed me. They didn't even know that anything was wrong. Some speakers begin their presentation by saying that they want a conversation with the audience rather than giving a formal speech. The secret is to go with who you are. Some speakers like a podium and formality. Others are more comfortable literally moving into the audience for interaction." Feed your strengths and starve your weaknesses until you gain enough confidence to address such weaknesses.

It is also wise to arrive early at the site where you are giving your presentation so that you experience the physical setting. What is the size of the room? What is the seating arrangement? Do you have the kind of equipment that you want to use and the electrical outlets and extension cords you need? What is the lighting like? Are there any distractions, such as a gurgling coffee pot or thin walls that will not keep out noise from rooms next door? Arriving early will give you the chance to make changes in the physical setting and also relax as much as possible.

Perhaps the most important thing you can do in presenting yourself is to share stories of real life experiences that illustrate points you wish to make. These stories have an authenticity that will get and hold an audience's attention.

Please use the following blank space to take notes on how you have experienced anxiety before and/or during presentation of self activities-on your part or on the part of others. How have you coped with such anxiety? How do you react to ways suggested in this essay? [See Resources D & G.]

A POPEYE

Moment

Springtime arrived in our high school, the time when all teachers must be on alert! The trees start to bloom, hormones are bubbling and students are getting ready for spring break. The principal, while walking down the hall in our one-floor school building, saw a manhole cover lift, and a senior boy and girl emerged from the short ladder below. The principal took the couple to his office and reprimanded them for being where they shouldn't be. He then turned on the public address system and announced that any students using the tunnels underneath the school would face serious consequences. You can, of course, guess what happened in the days that followed. Several students rose to the occasion and developed a sophisticated system for exploring the tunnels under the school. Their success in this enterprise was the talk of the school.

Shortly after this, there was a faculty meeting where the matter of students smoking behind the school was discussed. The principal suggested that male faculty members volunteer to stand on top of the school building at the rear of the school in order to take pictures of the offenders. This plan was discarded when no volunteers stepped forward to accept the invitation.

Students returned from spring break with more high jinks in mind. They hung the principal in effigy from the flagpole in front of the school. The principal, in a move interpreted by faculty members to be either ingenious or stupid, took the effigy down and placed it in the chair behind his desk for the remainder of the day.

The final assembly of the school year was held in the gym in April. The city symphony, known for its excellence, performed while students sat in the bleachers. During their second selection, a small group of boys started dropping heavy textbooks from a corner in the top of the bleachers to the gym floor-THUMP, THUMP, THUMP! I quickly surveyed the gym to see which faculty members were there to monitor the students. I was surprised that the principal, the assistant principal and I were the only three adults in attendance. Other faculty members were in their classrooms, the faculty lounge or who knows where else. There was obviously no system in place for monitoring students in assemblies. Because of the bleacher arrangement, it took several minutes before two of us adults in attendance could make our way to the student offenders to check their behavior.

Since the assembly was at the end of the school day, the student offenders were taken to the principal's office, and the rest of the students left the school campus. I returned it to my classroom, sat down at my desk and wrote on a piece of paper: *I CAN'T STANDS IT NO MORE!* I had reached my *Popeye Moment.* This was the moment when Popeye, one of the most famous comic strip characters ever drawn, can't take any more from his antagonist. What were my options? I could resign, give leadership where and when possible to trying to change the present chaotic culture of the school, be passive-aggressive, or try to ride it out, hoping for new leadership at the top. Two weeks later the principal announced he would take early retirement at the end of the school year A first-rate principal from another school system in the state was appointed, and a core group of the faculty, including myself, began the challenging but rewarding work of creating a better school culture.

Please use the following blank space to describe Popeye moments that you have faced and how you dealt with them. If you were to return to these situations today, what would you do differently if anything? Also describe any such moments you face today and what you plan to do about them. [See Resources F & H.]

TALKING TO
Parents

Reading Frank McCourt's *Teacher Man* (2005) is a treat because he takes the reader backstage into the real life of a teacher. For example, he reveals some of the hidden secrets about what is missing from teacher education: "No one ever told me how to handle parents on Open School Day." (P. 70). He added: "I said positive things about all my students. They were attentive, punctual, considerate, eager to learn and everyone of them had a bright future and the parents should be proud. Dad and Mom would look at each other and smile and say, See? or they'd be puzzled and say, You talkin' about our kid? Our Harry?" (P. 71). He describes many humorous examples of what happened on Open School Day.

We were curious about why teacher education doesn't prepare teachers to talk to parents on Open House Night or Walk the Schedule Night. The result is a book titled *The Charismatic Leader: The Presentation of Self and the Creation of Educational Settings* (2006). The book begins with a cautionary tale about a ninth-grade algebra class. Parents walked the schedules of their children. The teacher in each class began with a ten-minute presentation followed by a five-minute question-and-answer period. The whole process seemed to be fairly routine until a parent entered Mr. Jones ninth-grade algebra class. His opening remarks were somewhat interesting, but it was the question-and-answer session that caught the attention of the 20 parents in attendance. A bright and articulate mother raised her hand and said, "Mr. Jones, how will this ninth-grade algebra class help my child when he is in high school and college?" It was the body language of the audience that demonstrated their personal interest in the question and its impending answer. They leaned forward and all eyes and ears awaited Mr. Jones' answer. "I have no earthly idea," Mr. Jones responded. A collective gasp followed, after which the parents filed out of the classroom.

The remainder of *The Charismatic Leader* describes a program that professional development leaders and teacher educators can use to bring attention to relating to parents in general and talking to parents in particular. The civilities of leadership, what we call "the table manners of leadership," are of special importance. For example, successful leaders are adept in setting the stage for more substantive conversation by using small talk that establishes an affinity connection. Such talk relaxes parents and invites them to speak.

It is our view that the teacher as professional is able to explain to others, parents in particular in this case, what they are doing and why. Doing this well conveys teacher competence and instills confidence in the teacher's ability to articulate ideas. Listening and writing are other skills that can have a significant influence on parents. Personal comments about a child's progress and challenges make it clear to parents that the teacher knows about and cares about their child. One thing for sure is that we have a long way to go in learning more about how teachers and other adults in the school can communicate better with parents.

Please use the following blank space to write notes about your reactions to this essay. Were you given opportunities and instruction in your teacher education and professional development experiences for talking to parents during open houses at school? How have you learned what you have learned on this subject? What can you and your colleagues do to give attention to this subject? [See Resources E & G.]

Quick Fixes

Andrea Mitchell (2005), one of the most watched, most respected television reporters for more than a quarter of a century, interviewed presidential advisor, Brent Scrowcroft, in an effort to better understand intelligence breakdowns leading up to 9/11 and he told her: "We're getting to the point where our ability to collect information far exceeds our ability to analyze it. We need some help" (p. 343). If we look at our own lives as teachers, we recognize the validity of Scrowcroft's remarks. We have information overload.

A natural response to this reality is to seek the quick fix. We adopt a bumper sticker mentality in trying to address very complex issues. Our culture of busyness supports a quick fix approach to information overload: "There isn't time for long conversations with psychiatrists. Take a pill." "You have a colleague who annoys you. Tell him or her to 'SNAP OUT OF IT!'" "You need objectives for lesson plans and accrediting institutions? Just call this number in California and use plastic to get them."

Reflection appears to be a luxury of the unemployed. A teacher, who is also the mother of three children, shared her plight: "I spend my spare time in a van taking kids to music lessons, gymnastics, soccer, swimming, tennis, dance and church activities. Then I rush home to get dinner, clean the house and do the laundry. It is little wonder that my kids sometimes say to me, 'I just want to stay home and do what I want to do.' Everything is scheduled these days."

Today's culture seems to work against passing on traditions and activities that take time to learn and don't provide immediate gratification. Some parents believe that gifts to children will win their approval and buy them space from parenting. Tracy Kidder (1999) has a character in his book, *Home Town,* whose "wealth helped him to secure that kindness, through what he called 'premptive bribery'" (p. 119). A teacher, who loved sailing, didn't believe in this practice and took his own children and their friends to a nearby lake to teach them navigational skills and instill in them the same love for the sport that he had. His children's friends immediately went into the cabin of the boat and started playing electronic games with the sailor's children.

The challenge for us as teachers is to demonstrate a balance between the best of the past with an understanding of the present. Our love for ideas and recognition of the distinction between what can be quickly fixed and what can't serve as an example for those we lead. And, we can help others understand that most problems are part of larger dilemmas. For example, getting chalk from the supply cabinet is a problem that can be easily solved, but there will always be more needs and desires than available resources.

Please use the following blank space to note your response to this essay. How have you experienced the issues presented in the essay? What efforts have you made as a teacher to make a distinction between problems that can be quickly fixed and larger dilemmas that we try to reconcile? What has resulted from such efforts? [See Resource I.]

SCHOOL AS AN

Oasis

Mike Yankoski (2004) captures what many of us feel when experiencing serious difficulties in our lives in his moving book titled *Under The Overpass:* "For some reason, I hardly ever admitted when things weren't going well. Instead, I usually glossed over my struggles with an easy cliché like 'it's all good' or 'hanging in there' and thought nothing of it" (p. 45). When Joyce, a teacher, read this excerpt from Yankoski's book, assigned in a graduate school class, she took it to heart and wrote about it in her professional autobiography as follows: "I really identified with this passage in the book. It provoked me to explore why I don't share with others, particularly in the school where I teach, some of the problems I face in life. One reason is that I was told in one of my teacher education classes that I shouldn't let my personal life get in the way of my professional responsibilities. Another reason is that I don't want to burden my friends at work with my personal problems. Perhaps the most important reason why I don't take my problems to work with me is that I want to look strong rather than weak. I especially don't want my colleagues to patronize me by coming up to me and saying, 'Are you ok?' 'Are you feeling better today?' When some people do this, I have the feeling that they enjoy my being in a weaker position than they are."

Joyce added the following to her story: "Last year, I had some medical problems, including breast cancer. I didn't want to return to school until I was completely ok. I wanted to act and look like things in my life were absolutely normal. This way of thinking was interrupted by a sermon I heard in our church on how we feel we are in the wilderness when we face difficulties, and we stay away from the church at the very time when it can be an oasis where we can heal faster. Upon hearing this, I decided that my teaching and school could also serve as an oasis that would help me heal faster. Sharing with my trusted colleagues at work was one of the most helpful parts of my recovery. And helping children learn kept my mind off of my problems. I discovered through all of this that trying to be 'Super Woman' and trying to control everything was too heavy a burden to carry."

M. Scott Peck (1978) relates the benefits of new understandings like those acquired by Joyce: "What they once perceived as problems they now perceive as opportunities. What were once loathsome barriers are now welcome challenges. Thoughts previously unwanted become helpful insights; feelings previously disowned become sources of energy and guidance. Occurrences that once seemed to be burdens now seem to be gifts, including the very symptoms from which they have recovered" (p. 296).

Please use the following blank space to take notes. Can you identify with what Joyce learned about school and teaching as an oasis when confronting difficulties in your personal life? What have you learned about this matter in your own experiences or from observing and talking to colleagues and others? If this essay contains new insights, what is your plan for doing something to implement these insights? [Resource F.]

I YAM WHAT

I Yam...

Lee and Dwight were friends in college who keep in touch as they continue in their careers in education. Lee loves teaching high school mathematics and respectfully declined offers by some of his principals to become a school administrator. Dwight, on the other hand, knew almost from his first day as a teacher that he wanted to move into administration at the first available opportunity. His principals mentored him, and he left teaching for an assistant principalship in a middle school after two years in the classroom. Two years later, he became the principal of his middle school. Both Lee and Dwight have a strong sense of self and are respected by their colleagues for the individuals they are.

After two years as a middle school principal, Dwight was appointed principal of the largest high school in his district. During the summer after his third year as a high school principal, Dwight faced a serious situation. He needed an excellent teacher to teach advanced courses in mathematics. He had just lost one of his best math teachers to a large insurance company that wanted an actuarial expert with a strong math background.

Dwight knew that his chances of getting a first-rate math teacher at this late date in the year were slim to none. He immediately thought of Lee as an excellent candidate for this position. Lee's track record as a math teacher would make him an easy sell to central administration and the personnel office. Since Lee lived in a nearby town, he and his family would not have to move and Dwight was in a position to give Lee a handsome raise in salary.

Dwight phoned Lee and asked him if he was interested in the position. Lee indicated that he was and would meet with his friend the next day in Dwight's office. Dwight greeted Lee the next day and spelled out in some detail the fine opportunity the new position would give Lee. He explained the details of the contract, such as salary, advanced courses to teach and instructional support from the chair of the math department and others. They were both excited about the terms of the agreement and felt that their trust and respect for each other would make this opportunity work with no problems-particularly in a school of this size. At the end of their conversation, Dwight turned to Lee and said: "There is one other thing I should add. I will give you all the protection you need to be successful." Lee said that he would need to talk with his family before signing the contract. They agreed to meet the next day to finalize their verbal agreement.

As Lee rode home in his car, he was puzzled by Dwight's final comment about protection. He talked with his wife well into the night about what Dwight might have meant by this comment. After the usual introductory civilities during their meeting in Dwight's office the next day, Lee said that he felt he needed to talk very candidly about his reservations concerning Dwight's offer to give protection: "Dwight, the best way I can respond to your comment about giving me protection is to quote from one of my favorite comic book characters, Popeye-"I YAM WHAT I YAM, AND THAT'S ALL I YAM." By this I mean that I respect myself too much as a person to want protection. Is there something going on here that I need to know about?"

Dwight was obviously taken aback by Lee's statements and noted that they were given with a good deal of conviction and with some nervousness. Dwight apologized for his statement the previous day and added: "I'm afraid that I fell into the rescuer's trap as an administrator. I have been reminded by a friend or two that with authority comes the inclination to control situations that don't need to be controlled-largely to feed my own ego. I respect your ability to take care of yourself and I will remind myself to honor this when you join our faculty."

Lee thanked Dwight for his candor and apology and they both seemed relieved when their relationship seemed to return to normal. Lee then accepted the position.

Please use the following blank space to critique this situation: review it, adopt a point-of-view and support this point-of-view. Does this story have the ring of truth? If you were in Lee's position, what would you have done? Have you faced situations like this and if so, what did you do? [See Resources C & J.]

PRIVATE

Victories

Jaime's story is one we have heard from a number of teachers in different parts of our country and it deserves to be told in her own words. "When I was in teacher education classes in college, some of our professors told us that once our classroom door is closed we can create our own world. This promise was one that I looked forward to, as I am an independent person who doesn't like to have someone looking over my shoulder all of the time, telling me what to do. What I didn't realize is that there is a downside to all of this. Teaching can be a lonely profession. There are those wonderful times in the classroom when I try something different or teach a well-prepared lesson that really works, and I want to share with other teachers and the principal how happy I am about my success. But I've discovered in staff development workshops that other teachers are reluctant to celebrate successes. When a first-year teacher excitedly told the story of how something she did worked out so well, a few teachers rolled their eyes, and I quickly discovered that this is something that you don't do. The principal is so busy that I don't feel comfortable talking to her about things that go well in my teaching. It sounds like bragging. I have come to the point where I see that my victories are largely private ones."

Mentoring programs and teaching teams can be very helpful in speaking to Jaime's needs, and yet it still remains true that many, if not most, victories a teacher experiences are private ones. This is the case, even though it is a very American phenomenon to want public acclaim and appreciation for our good work. And, some colleagues, particularly those with an eye for administrative positions, have finely honed strategies for calling attention to their accomplishments. They participate in anticipatory socialization, the acting out of the administrative role even though they are presently teachers. Their main audience is administrators who are in a position to hire them rather than their teacher colleagues.

With time and maturity, we hopefully begin to realize that large dramatic events in our lives often lack depth and don't last very long. Actor Richard Dreyfuss talks about this realization: "It's thrilling. I enjoy even doing little things that I disdained before, like color-coordinating what I'm wearing, not looking like a jerk. It's the simple pleasure of behaving like a normal human being" (Dreyfuss, 1986, p. 6). I observed this in how much grandchildren enjoyed being with their grandmother as they made and decorated cookies over the holidays and how delighted the grandchildren were in walking through a field with their grandfather as he identified and described wildflowers and birds.

Teacher leaders are challenged to create more humane and caring school cultures in which victories can be shared and celebrated. It is in such environments that we learn from each other and discover in ourselves and our students talents that were previously unrecognized.

Please use the blank space that follows to note what you have learned as a teacher about private victories in relation to public celebrations of the good work that teachers do, including your own good work. How can you give good leadership in dealing with this subject in your school? [See Resource F.]

NEVER

Satisfied?

I was well into my third year of teaching and started feeling like I was finding my sound as a teacher-in a good groove and reasonably comfortable. Our school culture was taking shape and the principal, appointed in the fall of the year, and the faculty were functioning well as a team. There was just one thing that bothered me about this new principal: He was the kind of person who never seemed satisfied with what we did, no matter how much we improved. It always seemed like he would put a zinger in at the end of his formative evaluations of our teaching: "I liked the class interaction but you can still involve more students in class discussions. Have you thought of using different seating arrangements so that students in the back move to the front and can't hide out as much as a few of them do?" His comments weren't limited to the classroom: "You have the talent to be a faculty leader. I would like to see you head some of our committees rather than simply being a committee member."

Mary, the assistant superintendent in charge of curriculum and instruction, was a person I trusted and respected, and we occasionally saw each other at volleyball games where our middle-school daughters were on the same team. She asked me how things were going at our school, and I said "Fine, except for the fact that no matter what I do the principal never seems to be satisfied and treats me like I'm not good enough." I added, "I know that I may sound like I'm having a pity party, but you asked and this is the way I feel."

Mary turned to me and said in a pleasant voice, "Isn't it wonderful that your principal hasn't given up on you!" "What do you mean by that?" I responded with a surprised tone of voice. Mary answered with a smile on her face: "Some leaders accept what people do as the starting AND finishing place. They are warm and fuzzy, but they don't get the best out of those they lead. They don't set the bar high enough for some teachers and have given up on others. They leave you with the feeling that they are just happy to be principals." She added, "Does your principal expect more of you than he does of himself? Is he willing to work toward his own improvement as much as he wants you to work toward improving?" I answered with a sheepish grin on my face: "Yes, he really does. He arrives at school early, stays late and never asks more of us than he is willing to give himself." Mary then said: "The way he shares his expectations is important. He doesn't strike me as a preachy, judgmental, critical parent type of person."

Mary and I then dropped the subject to return to watching the game. At first, I wasn't sure I liked what she said, but strangely enough, she had given me a different perspective on my principal, and it was a kind of turning point in the way I viewed and related to him. Rather than being annoyed at some of his comments about my teaching and leadership, I smiled to myself and thought back to my conversation at the volleyball game with Mary. And, I appreciated how Mary had a smile on her face and used her sense of humor to convey her message to me. I would appreciate more favorable comments from my principal but I do see his leadership style in a larger perspective now.

Recently I read a book on Red Auerbach, considered by some as the greatest professional basketball coach we've had. Red was asked about John Wooden, UCLA coach who won ten national titles. Red responded: "I hear people say all the time that he had great talent, which he certainly did. Well, there's two things about that: One, you gotta get the talent. That's part of the job. Two, when you get it you gotta make sure you don't screw it up. A lot of coaches-I mean a lot take great talent and screw it up. Wooden took good players and made them very good; very good ones and made them great; and great ones and made them greater. That's coaching" (Auerbach & Feinstein, 2004, p. 225).

Please use the following blank space to note any reactions you have to this essay. Have you had the feelings conveyed to Mary about some leaders always expecting more of you and leaving you with the feeling that they think you are never good enough? How do you react to these leaders and situations? What do you think of Mary's response? What kind of leader are you in this regard? What changes, if any, do you want to make in your leadership style in light of your answers to the previous questions?

NEGLECTING SCHOOL
History

The newly appointed principal of our school has no experience as a teacher or school administrator. He is a recently retired military leader whose success in the military gained him his position as principal via lateral entry. He will now take required courses to become fully certified. We expected him to continue to use some military language, but we were unprepared for the way he greeted us in the first faculty meeting: "Welcome aboard," he said in a self-assured voice, after which he told us something about his previous experience in the military, and shared his vision for what he referred to as *my* school. After his brief speech a colleagues turned to me and whispered, "I thought it was *our* school."

After sharing this story with teachers in our seminars across the country, we asked participants if they could identify with this situation. Somewhat to our surprise, person after person told stories about how they have been greeted by newly appointed principals and superintendents in a similar manner. One person in a seminar said, "We are left with the feeling that our school or school system has no history or no history of any value. It was as if the new hire thought the school or school system began with his or her entrance."

We believe that it takes a good deal of ego to accept a position as school or school-system leader, but we also think that more than this comes to play in the story. History is often neglected in our society and culture because it is an annoyance. Our brand of capitalism, for example, knocks down building after building, after which construction of a new supermarket or restaurant begins immediately. When leaders leave a position, it seems like a waste of resources to give much attention to what previous leaders did or did not do. We want a quick fix, and easy answers keep us from studying history. "Just do it" is our mantra. "Where there are no alternatives, the wise man has said, there are no problems" (Buckley, 1970, p. 14). Knowing history generates alternatives.

When Red Auerbach said he would visit a recruit for the Boston Celtics, he was advised to bring his championship rings to establish his credibility or the kid wouldn't know who he was. "Red laughed. He understands how it is with today's generation of players. He also understands that players in college today were born fifteen to twenty years after he stopped coaching. 'Most of them don't remember Russell or Cousy or

Havlicek or the Jones boys, much less remember me,' he will say. 'That's okay. I understand. They all think basketball started with Michael Jordan.' Actually, with Jordan now retired, a lot of the current players think basketball began with Kobe Bryant. Or LeBron James" (Auerbach & Feinstein, 2004, p. 250).

Please use the following blank space to note how your newly appointed school principals relate to the history of your schools. Do they honor this history? Ignore it? What do you do or think should be done in the event that this issue is important to you? Does the story told in this issue have "the ring of truth"? Why or why not? [See Resource B.]

THE TIPPING

Point

When I began teaching, my right-brain orientation resisted a linear-sequential (left-brain) approach to curriculum and instruction. My rationale for this orientation was that a creative teacher would not have a predetermined curriculum but would instead have faith in an emerging curriculum-a curriculum that would benefit both students and their teacher. The effective teacher would know his or her subject matter, of course, but enthusiasm for learning would serve as a catalyst for constructing curriculum. It didn't take too long for me to discover that *ALL* students didn't share my right-brain orientation. A few students would candidly approach me and say things like, "I'm just beginning to understand what you want us to do and learn, and I wish I had known this from the beginning of the year." After hearing these comments enough, I decided to experiment with some more linear, sequential approaches to teaching. For example, I would distribute a copy of goals and objectives, list learning activities, and include evaluation procedures for units of study. What a surprise to see how my left-brain learners appreciated this simple change in my instruction! An even bigger surprise was that my right-brain students also reacted favorably to this change.

Armed with this success, I started keeping a brief summary of progress, in outline form, each day and distributed photocopies of this to students at appropriate times. Lo and behold, the main benefactor of this innovation was me-the teacher. It kept me on track and also encouraged me to make mid-course corrections that were helpful. An unintended consequence was that I appeared to be well-organized, something that was especially noted by left-brain colleagues and administrators. There were, however, some odd remarks by a few right-brain colleagues, who felt I had abandoned their ship and fled to the enemy's camp: "What a control freak you've become!" "You're just trying to look good for the bean counters." "Who are you trying to impress?"

As I look back on my transformation in trying to achieve more balance between predetermined curriculum and emerging curriculum, as well as structure and flexibility, I realize that a number of little things led to the tipping point, that place where I reframed the way I viewed the world of curriculum and instruction. I actively listened to the comments of my students and attended to some of the smallest details in order to reach this tipping point. These changes were clearest to me in reading a book by Malcolm Gladwell (2002), titled *The Tipping Point: How Little things Can Make a Big Difference.* (See pp. 123-124 & 257).

Please use the following blank space to take notes in order to critique this essay. What is your primary orientation to teaching and learning-left-brain or right-brain? Have you adjusted your teaching to accommodate the opposite orientation of your own? If so, what happened to you in the process? If not, why not? What do you think will happen if you do make this change? Please use these same questions in assessing your colleagues' teaching. [See Resources H, I, & J.]

IN MY OWN
Way

Alan Watts, philosopher and author of books on world religions, wrote a wonderful autobiography titled *In My Own Way* (1972). The double meaning in this title has important implications for teachers and teaching. Do I do it in my own way, or do I get in my own way? Effective teaching always seems like a balancing act as we try to honor the independence or autonomy of each person, including ourselves, while at the same time giving fair play to ways in which we relate to each other and the environment. When we are too self-centered, we get in our own way, and when we are too focused on relationships, our individual selves can be lost.

Yo-Yo Ma, brilliant cellist, was asked about mental and physical preparations for his four and a half hour concert where he played six Bach suites. He answered: "You are so into the music that you don't control it anymore. You are led by it." He added, "Bach takes you to a very quiet place within yourself, to the inner core, a place where you are calm and at peace" (Friedrich, 1991, p. 99). This captures the artistry of teaching, or any artistic expression for that matter. We are so involved in the creative process that we lose track of time and have a sense of awe, wonder and amazement. We are alive!

It is impossible for us as teachers to have this feeling all of the time but this is precisely the point. We celebrate these creative moments because they are in such contrast to other times. It is during these creative moments that we see life in the eyes of our students, and classroom discipline takes care of itself. It is the opposite of those times when we are so control oriented that we become paralyzed by teaching techniques and analysis. A Zen poem describes self-conscious contexts in which we get in our own way:

> There was a centipede on the road,
> And when confronted by a toad.
> Was asked which foot came after which,
> This worked his mind to such a pitch,
> He lay distracted in a ditch.

The challenge as a teacher is to have enough structure and consistency so that students and the teacher have the comfort of knowing where they stand and what is expected of them, but not so much structure that it curbs creativity and freedom to express selves. The difficulty of the challenge is that it is something that teachers and their students have to work on much of the time. It is like adjusting to an ocean's tides. We end up moving our beach chairs, as there is no one enduring or right place to sit.

We find Frank McCourt's *Teacher Man* (2005) a compelling book to read because it is a memoir about his thirty-year teaching career, during which he, like Yo-Yo Ma, tried to find his sound. There was no quest for certainty on their part, but there was love and respect for the artistic expression of teaching on Frank McCourt's part and love and respect for the artistic expression of playing the cello by Yo-Yo Ma.

Please use the following blank space to describe those moments when you felt that you were totally connected with artistic expression as a teacher. What feelings did you have during these times? What did you see in your students during these times? How have you worked to achieve a balance between autonomy and working with others in your own life? In allowing and encouraging this in the lives of your students? [See Resource F.]

Never

TOO LATE TO CATCH UP

Lee was a curious child observant of everything around him. Without saying anything about it to others, he would sit in the children's choir each Sunday morning, watching and thinking about what adults did. He noted that Bill Lutz, an FBI agent, was an imposing figure in the adult choir and wondered what life as an agent was like for him during the week. He also observed that Fred Lutz, Bill's brother, who also sang in the adult choir, was a loving husband and father to his children. Lee concluded, "That's the kind of husband and father I want to be some day."

Sports in general and basketball and tennis were Lee's main interests as a teenager, with academics a distant second. In fact, the best thing we can say about Lee's academic life in high school and first two years of college is that he didn't burn out. At the beginning of Lee's junior year in college, Lee began thinking about teaching and he discovered a love for ideas in his courses in history, philosophy, religion, drama and literature. He approached one professor asking for advice as to what he should read in order to catch up. His English professor responded, "At this point, young man, anything will do!"

Lee followed this professor's advice and discovered in reading many different authors that their writing styles had a musical quality to them. Words and cadences, for example, were like instruments in their hands Fortunately, thanks to his mother, Lee had been introduced to lessons on the piano, and his father arranged for him to study the clarinet with Marius Fossenkemper, principal clarinetist with the Detroit Symphony. Lee came to see that reading with a discerning eye was like soap and water for writers-an essential part of their craft. He learned to listen to the emotional resonance of ideas, and in turn, to share such resonance with others through his own writing.

When Lee entered student teaching, he became conscious that he was on a kind of mission to help his students discover how one's love for learning and ideas could last a lifetime. He celebrated how his early childhood talents as an observer of life could be merged with his newfound love for teaching. Pat Conroy (2002), famous author, captured what Lee had learned in describing his best basketball coach: "Good coaching is good teaching and nothing else"(p. 106).

Please use the following blank space to describe how you identify with Lee's discoveries about one's love for learning, ideas and life itself. Tell your own story in your own words so that others will see how it is never too late to learn what Lee experienced. [See Resource J.]

BEING
Evaluated

One of the most challenging aspects of teaching is what to do about teacher evaluations. Evaluations, usually by principals, range from benign neglect to micromanaging. During the first three years of my teaching, our principal wrote the same evaluative sentence: "He does a nice job with boys and girls." My first reaction to this benign neglect was, "What a relief to not have any negative comments!" My second response was, "What in the world does this sentence mean?" I checked with a fellow teacher and he said, "Just give thanks that the principal didn't take this any more seriously than he did. Go back to work knowing that what you are doing is acceptable in his eyes." I had the nagging feeling, however, that the principal didn't take the teacher evaluation process seriously, and as a result, I wasn't especially appreciated for my good work by him and couldn't make any mid-course corrections that would improve my teaching.

The benign neglect approach to teacher evaluation still exists in some places but No Child Left Behind legislation's two most controversial provisions, the Reading First program and the "highly qualified teachers" mandate, have been implemented by the U.S. Department of Education in a highly prescriptive way. Narrowly defined reading instruction and the demand that teachers demonstrate subject-matter knowledge have amounted to a kind of micro-management with the medical model as their justification. At the same time, many school and school-system administrators encourage teachers to show their competence by using whatever works, a pragmatic constructivist approach to teaching, learning and evaluation. Michael J. Petrilli (2006) states: "Is it any surprise that educators feel whipsawed between competing demands? On the one hand, the federal government is saying to do whatever works to boost student learning, and on the other hand it's saying to do things in a certain prescribed, preapproved way" (p. 36).

What is a teacher to do about this battle between *what works and whatever works?* It is our view that the teacher as a professional should know the issues involved in teacher and student evaluation, think through and adopt a point of view or thesis with regard to these issues and be able to articulate this view to fellow professionals, as well as others interested in education. Doing this isn't always easy but you won't be faulted for not knowing the issues involved, taking a stand and supporting it. You will be secure in the knowledge that you are a professional who knows the game and the score.

Please use the blank space that follows to record your reactions to this essay. How have you been evaluated as a teacher and by whom? Have you been satisfied with assessments of your effectiveness as a teacher? Why or why not? What do you think needs to be done to have more effective teacher evaluations? [See Resources I & J.]

AUTHORITY, INFLUENCE AND

Accountability

Dee is a third-year teacher leader who describes herself as a leader in the middle: "I have what one of my professors calls 'amorphous anxiety'. I am pressured by the principal to raise test scores, and I know and understand that she is pressured by federal and state governments to standardize education. Mandates are the order of the day. At the same time, teachers I lead want me to be compassionate about the stress they feel as a result of test mania. In one of my graduate classes, we have identified a number of questions that speak to the anxiety that most of us in education feel: In whose interest is it to attach numbers to student learning and standardize curricula? Why is it that those with authority don't involve those of us who are being assessed in determining how we are assessed? Why is it that those with authority continue to expand their power and make our schools more and more bureaucratic? What can we do to influence politicians and other decision-makers?"

We begin to address Dee's dilemma by defining some important terms. *Authority,* with regard to education, is usually taken to mean power that is delegated or assigned to a person or persons in an organizational setting. *Influence* refers to unofficial power to make something happen or to keep something from happening. It is often directed at those with more formal power or authority. We shouldn't make the mistake of equating power with truth. Those with power want to see their policies and agendas realized. *Accountability* is one's ability to explain or justify ones actions. It raises questions like: "By whom?" "To Whom?" "And, in what way(s)?" It is important to note that accountability alone won't fix anything. You have to have a plan, and you have to work the plan: know what you love or have a passion for, and know what you are willing to give up to realize your plan. If you do this, you will move from intentions to reality.

These questions and more like them are central to education and educators in this country as well as some other countries. Much of the rhetoric surrounding these matters is of the bumper-sticker variety-an effort by politicians and others to reduce complex issues to simple formulas that serve political purposes. Ironically, at the very time that schools and schooling are becoming more and more technical and bureaucratic, Ken Greer, CEO of Greer & Associates, shared the following with Tom Friedman, author of the best-selling book, *The World Is Flat* (2005): "Everyone can see what everyone else is doing now, and everyone has the same tools, so you have to be the very best, the most creative thinker" (p. 344). He adds: "It used to be about what you were able to do. Clients would say, 'Can you do this?' 'Can you do that?' Now it's much more about the creative flair and personality you can bring to the assignment. It's all about imagination" (p. 325).

How can you as teachers and educational leaders reconcile this dilemma so that you can inspire students and colleagues? Teachers and administrators tell us that there is no substitute for realistically assessing and taking a stand with regard to the status quo. "What is being done?" confronts "What do you think should be done?" "What can be done?" emerges from the first two questions. It is our hope that other essays in this book will help you answer these questions in a more specific manner.

Charles Kimball (2002) relates one of the most important principles with regard to this important topic: "The more the power and authority are focused in one or a few people, the higher the likelihood of abuse" (p. 94). He adds: "It is all too easy to get swept up in the emotional wake of a charismatic leader or a compelling idea. Blind obedience to individuals or to doctrines is never wise. Such behavior effectively abdicates individual responsibility, and as we have observed, that can be dangerous" (p. 96). We are also reminded that mature persons find authority in themselves. We often learn this in dealing with appointed authorities who are insensitive, incompetent or both. Pat Conroy (2002) discovered this in playing for his basketball coach at The Citadel: "As we took to the court for the second half, I made a secret vow to myself that I would never listen to a single thing that Mel Thompson said to me again. I would obey him and honor him and follow him, but I would not let him touch the core of me again. He was my coach, but I was my master" (p. 185).

Madeleine Albright, the first woman to occupy the secretary of state position, reminds us in *The Mighty and the Almighty* (2006) that "leaders need to have confidence in themselves, but there is a fine line between confidence and self-righteousness" (p. 163). Authentic education, teaching and learning, encourage critical thinking and responsible action. Warmth, compassion and common sense offer more virtue than blind obedience to one dogma or another. These reminders are a beginning place as we continue to address Dee's dilemma as the person in the middle.

Please use the following space to record your views of the relationship between authority, influence and accountability. How do the questions and issues raised in this essay speak to what you experience each day in your school and/or school system? What questions remain in your mind on these important issues of authority, influence and accountability? [See Resources C & I.]

Graduate

SCHOOL AS AN OASIS

Joan lingered near the front of the graduate school classroom. This was her second class with me as her professor, and we had established a relationship based on trust and respect for each other's abilities. She said to me, "Graduate school is an oasis for me at this point in my life and career." No graduate student had ever used this metaphor to describe graduate school, and so I asked her what she meant by this. She responded: "Graduate school is a pleasant relief from the pressures of school, family and other community activities. Each Tuesday night I come to the university for three hours, and I can focus on my own interests. There is so much pressure at my school to get test scores up and close the achievement gap that I don't have the freedom to do the creative kinds of teaching I did when I started teaching. After school, I haul my kids around town to get them to dance class, gymnastics, swimming lessons and soccer practice and games. Then I rush home to cook dinner, do the laundry and clean the house. Graduate school also gives me an excuse to be by myself at home in order to read and write papers assigned by my professors. I have all of my stuff on the dining room table, as the table is only used for holiday dinners anyway. When I work on papers, I sometimes put that yellow tape used by police and fire departments around the chairs at the table so that nobody disturbs my work. My family laughed at this at first, but they got the idea that this is my space. I also have some new friends in graduate school, teachers from other schools in this area of the state, and we share stories with each other. This gives me perspective on what other teachers do in their schools and school systems, and I feel emotional support for the personal and professional problems I face. We also celebrate successes, sometimes going to a nearby restaurant after class. When I was an undergraduate student, I treated most of my classes as hurdles that had to be jumped over in order to get a degree, but in graduate school I am taking my time to enjoy being part of a learning community. It is a different feeling-a real oasis for me. When I took my first course in graduate school I had little confidence and actually wondered if I would be able to do the work since it was some time since I received my bachelor's degree. I have built up my confidence now that I know that I can do the work and I am seeing connections between university learning and teaching that make my teaching more meaningful and even fun."

I thanked Joan for her insights, insights that gave me perspective on how important graduate school can be to working mothers and others-a kind of oasis in their lives. It struck me later that Joan has a real love for graduate school education at its best. I was also reminded of Mike Yankoski's statement that "real love always shows itself in action"(2005, p. 217). Joan had summoned up the courage to apply for graduate school and do the work needed to be an excellent student.

Please use the following blank space to take notes on how graduate school has influenced you. Have you found it to be the kind of oasis that Joan did? If you have not gone to graduate school yet, what do you expect it will be like? [See Resource F.]

A TEACHER'S INNER
Child

On the third Saturday of each month, seven of us get together for a two-hour lunch. We have done this for years, and as a result, we have come to know each other quite well. One of the things that makes our group interesting is that we have different occupations. I am the only teacher in the group. Our lunches begin with small talk, but it doesn't take long before we move into politics and religion. No subject is too controversial, and there is an unwritten rule that we will not cross the line to personally offend anyone in the group. Humor plays a key role in keeping this from happening.

It took some time for me to realize that one of the things that we have in common is that we have spent most of our adult lives trying to get what we think we didn't have in childhood. One person is a veterinarian who had few toys as a child, and he now has a host of miniature boats and cars that can be remotely controlled. Another member of our group, a businessman, is intensely involved in coaching little league sports teams, something that he didn't participate in as a player when he was a child. An attorney owns a farm and spends much of his spare time riding a tractor and building trails for his children's all terrain vehicles. He was raised in a large city as a child. A successful businessman, raised on a farm, is an avid tennis player and golfer, sports unavailable to him as a child. While I've worked my way up the ladder of car choices so that my next car, if all things go well, will be a luxury sports model.

At our last luncheon, I shared my view that one thing we have in common is using many of our resources to get what we didn't have as children. There was a pause in our conversation, after which there was a smile on nearly everyone's face followed by unanimous recognition that it was true. One fellow said, "It may not be the only driving force in my life but it certainly is a strong influence in my life. I'll admit it!"

Gloria Steinem (1992) writes about this phenomenon in her book titled *Revolution From Within: A Book of Self-Esteem:* "Each of us has an inner child of the past living within us. Those who needed to build no walls have access to that child's creativity and spontaneity. Those who had to leave this crucial core behind can tear down the walls, see what the child needed but didn't have, and begin to provide it now" (pp. 38-39). It is our challenge as teachers to mine this creativity and spontaneity.

Please use the space that follows to take notes on your reaction to this essay. Do you agree with the thesis that we spend much of our adult lives trying to have those things we didn't have as children? Please give examples from your own life as well as the lives of those you know to support or not support this thesis. How does your position with regard to this thesis influence how and what you teach? What do you want to do about this, if anything? [See Resource F.]

READING PEOPLE AS
Leaders

A teacher shared the following story with us: "Getting the right person in the right leadership role is one of the most important challenges in our school. This is especially true in our school, since leadership teams play a significant role. This year we were informed that a new position was being created. A member of our faculty will spend half time as a team leader/teacher and half time as the director of curriculum and instruction in the school as a whole. Our principal truly believes in shared decision-making, and I knew that she would be open to suggestions as to who should fill this position."

The story-teller continues: "As a mid-career teacher I have had considerable experience in reading people as to their leadership talents and leadership styles. Susan is one of our team leaders who is an excellent teacher and team leader, but she is the kind of person who has to be motivated by the right leaders in the school as a whole. She respects our principal but I am afraid that she will not be motivated if any of the other team leaders are assigned to the new position as director of curriculum and instruction. Susan is kind of eccentric and highly individualistic."

She adds: "After thinking about this situation, I decided to talk to the principal about my recommendation. I dropped by her office at the end of the school day and made my case: 'Susan respects you as a principal, is highly talented as a leader but has to be in a position where she respects the new director of curriculum and instruction. My recommendation to you is that you appoint Susan as the new director of curriculum and instruction. You can be sure that she will work hard for herself in this new position as she will be highly motivated.' The principal smiled and thanked me for my recommendation. The following week she appointed Susan as director of curriculum and instruction. The decision was a wise one, as Susan has gained the support and respect of the faculty and has demonstrated that she was an excellent choice for this position."

Bobby Knight, a controversial basketball coach to be sure, believes that Red Auerbach's decision to make Bill Russell the first African-American to coach a major professional team was one of his masterstrokes-but not for social or political reasons. Knight said, "It may have been one of the most brilliant moves ever made. When Red stopped coaching (the Boston Celtics), his biggest concern had to be figuring out a way to keep Russell motivated. Bill respected Red and played for him, but he wasn't necessarily going to do that for the next guy. But you could be damn sure that Russell would play hard *for Russell*" (Auerbach & Feinstein, 2004, p. 235).

Please use the following blank space to critique the rationale for recommending that Susan be appointed to the new position as director of curriculum and instruction. Do you think that you would have made the same decision that the principal made? If you disagree with the recommendation, state the case for this position?

Celebrating
TEAM MEMBERS

Teaching assistants are treated as lesser beings by some educators and others who are rank conscious. When they are included as contributing teaching team members, all kinds of good things can happen. The following narrative by a teaching assistant demonstrates this.

"A third-grade class had just completed watching the motivational *Math-a-Thon* video, which includes children at St. Jude Research Hospital thanking all who participate in order to raise money to help cure their cancers and other dreaded diseases. Then Patrice Reaves came into the room to teach the bi-weekly Latin lesson, this time formulated as a 'Roman style' picnic to teach the Latin words for the various foods she had brought with her, including juice to represent wine. After showing them how Romans toasted each other, she let them take turns proposing toasts. The first child raised her cup and toasted someone's birthday that day. Patrice echoed the toast ceremonially along with the rest of the class. Dekia stood up, raised her cup and said, 'This toast comes from the bottom of my heart-to the children of St. Jude!' To which Patrice, with no more or less recognition than the first toast, led the children in the repeat toast, 'To the children of St. Jude!' Patrice gave me, a teaching assistant, a passing smile, knowing I'm in charge of the Math-a-Thon at our school, but her equanimity with each child's toast gave no more credit to one over the other."

The teaching assistant added: "Patrice and I supported each other as a teaching team in a public way. Patrice was really wise not to play favorites with the children. She didn't say that one toast was better than the other. The classroom teacher also complimented us for our teamwork. All of us demonstrated our love and care for less-fortunate children at St. Jude by connecting what some might call an extracurricular activity with an in-class activity. Connecting the classroom and school with the outside world and supporting a worthwhile cause became part of our teaching team's purpose and activity. It is hard to express how important this is to me emotionally and professionally."

After 76 days adrift after his sailboat capsized in the Atlantic Ocean, Steven Callahan reached shore and asked himself, "What did I learn from the voyage?" He responded, "I have come to know that the fulfillment of goals is not enough in itself. It must be shared to be rewarding" (Callahan, 1986, p. 344).

Please use the following blank space to describe one or more activities you have been involved in as a team member to help persons in the world outside of the classroom. What were the benefits you experienced while doing this? What are some of the challenges you face in participating in these activities? [See Resource F.]

LAUGHTER AND THE JOY OF
Sharing

I sat in a barber's chair this morning and noticed a stoop-shouldered, somber-faced man open the door and walk slowly toward a chair where he waited to get a haircut. I estimated his age to be in the late eighties or early nineties. I said to myself, "Is this what it is like to get old and experience a life without emotion?" A few minutes later, two of his friends walked into the barber shop and sat next to him. They began kidding him about this and that, and before long, all three of them were laughing and carrying on about a time in the past when they put eggs in a backyard pen owned by a man who recently bought a rooster at a flea market. The three barbers and those of us who sat in their barber chairs joined in the conversation and laughter about Herb's rooster laying eggs. The climate in the barber shop was transformed. When the elderly man's turn came to get his haircut, he quickly got up from his chair and briskly walked to the barber's chair where he sat down with a big smile on his face. He, too, was transformed by laughter and the joy of sharing with others in community. I thought to myself, "This place has taken 20 to 30 years off his life in the matter of a few minutes."

This experience reminded me of times in the classroom when students and I were transformed by unplanned events that brought laughter and life to our learning community. And, I also remembered outside-of-school good times with students of a similar nature. I thought of how my lesson plans were sometimes interrupted by spontaneous events when students and I laughed and experienced the joy of sharing. As Patrick Welsh (1987) wrote in *Tales Out of School*: "The books on pedagogy stress the importance of control in the classroom. But it's often when things are a little out of control when I get a queasy feeling in my stomach that real learning takes place" (p. 24).

Please use the space that follows to record events you have experienced as an educator when laughter and the joy of sharing have taken place. What characterized these learning settings? For example, structure but also flexibility, the teacher didn't have to control everything going on, etc. [See Resources F & H.]

STRUCTURE AND
Flexibility

Bill loved being a wrestling coach and high school teacher. Although he was asked to apply for assistant principalships, he refused the offer and remained in his present teaching position for twenty years. During his exit interview after retiring, I asked him what the main thing was that he had learned over the years as a high school teacher. "I learned what to see and what not to see, what to do something about and what to ignore," he responded. I asked Bill for an example. His answer was most interesting: "I had rickets as a child and walk with a slight limp. Occasionally, a boy would mimic me after we walked past each other in the hall. When I began as a teacher, I would have him up against the wall and be in his face. I learned with time not to react to everything that annoyed me. I simply ignored some things and they went away. Giving them attention made them worse. I learned that the creative leader uses sources of power in a manner appropriate for a particular situation."

As the interview continued, I asked Bill what his views on structure, rules and flexibility were. His response was that of a seasoned leader: "Students, teachers and others need structure as it gives them comfort, security and a sense of direction. But structure, rules and a sense of order must be reasonable and adapted to particular cases. Paul, a good sized boy, arrived at school late one morning, and I confronted him about this matter. He responded in an angry manner. I talked with him outside my classroom door, and he said that his parents had told him over breakfast that they were getting a divorce. We continued to be in touch over the next few days and he became one of my strongest supporters. This situation reminded me of the power of listening. It also reminded me that I shouldn't confuse a dramatic event, such as punishing Paul in front of other students, with effective leadership."

Parker Palmer (2002) writes about the power of listening and says that "the teacher who connects more deeply with students and colleagues is likely to find his or her work life transformed." He adds, "When teachers reach out, they find themselves less lonely, less afraid, less exhausted, less bored, and more alive" (p. xxii).

Please use the blank space that follows to describe experiences you have had that speak to the matter of listening as a way to address reaching a balance between structure and flexibility. What problems have you experienced in trying to reach this balance? [See Resources F & G.]

A GOOD
Vacation

"Did you have a good vacation?" How many times have you heard this from colleagues after holidays during the teaching year and after time away from school in the summer! A classic assignment for students returning to school in the fall is to write an essay on your summer vacation.

The variety of answers you get from colleagues could fill a book: "It is good to be back and get my own kids in their schools again!" "It wasn't long enough!" "I missed the routine of work!" "It was a good break!"

Based on our own experiences as teachers and what teachers have told us about their own teaching, there are predictable patterns in the relationship between teaching and time off from teaching. First, retired teachers say that every day is Saturday now that they no longer teach, and vacations have little meaning because they are not a relief or change from work. In other words, vacations for teachers are an opportunity to do something different from their usual teaching routine. Second, getting away from work is a release from the stress and pressures of the responsibility of teaching, but anxiety kicks in once again as one approaches the time when the teacher has to return to work, no matter what kind of vacation is taken. Being with and often in front of students is stressful. Teaching is quite different from occupations where you have considerable life space and are not directly responsible for others from moment-to-moment. Third, many, if not most, teachers spend little time during the day with adults. Enter any department store and you will hear adult workers talking to each other about their personal problems. There is little time in teaching to share such personal matters with other adults, but vacation time does afford such contact. Fourth, vacations for teachers can give you a chance to consider the balance or lack of balance in your life between what you do and what you think you should do. Am I where I want to be in my career? Should I consider other career possibilities? What kinds of formal education will I need if I want to advance my career or change careers? How can I have more time to myself to do the things I want to do? What do I really want in life? What am I running away from? A host of questions can arise that are disquieting, and this prompts many teachers to be glad to return to the routine of the work world after a vacation.

"It is highly probable that as long as you teach, and you teach because of who you are, the best that you can hope for is to be *less unbalanced*. Your need to achieve, to master challenges, and to lead will always represent challenges to a balanced life style" (Brubaker & Coble, 2005, p. 80).

Please use the following blank space to note your responses to this essay. The question, "What is a good vacation?" is thought-provoking, and the essay simply opens the door for conversations you and your colleagues can have on this subject. Please participate in these discussions informally and in professional development sessions as your efforts to balance work and vacations are important personally and professionally. Use specific examples where possible. [See Resource F.]

Next Year

One of the things that you realize after teaching for a year or so is that a teacher's job is never done. You reach the end of the school year and vow to turn off school and teaching, but you just can't. You keep getting ideas and have a kind of "divine discontent" that drives you forward. This is true in any profession that values growth and development. Andrea Mitchell (2005), veteran television reporter, captures this in her book, titled *Talking Back:* "Above all, I felt that I was stretching myself, growing stronger and more confident as a correspondent. And the knowledge I had from covering foreign policy briefings and hearings on the Hill was now enriched by experience on the ground in all parts of the world" (pp. 259-260).

We have found that it can be useful to carry 3 by 5 inch cards on which we can write notes about new ideas for our own growth and development. We sometimes draw a rough picture of the setting we are in on the other side of the note card. Months, or even years after making the notation, we can return to the picture and be taken back to the place where we recorded an idea. Students and colleagues sometimes say things that are so important to our learning. If these comments are written down in their own words, they have special meaning.

The value of having the blank cards with us is that we never know when and where we will gain new insights-at a meeting, in a religious setting, in an airport, in the car, at a civic or sports event, etc. Our notations may also be useful if we decide to write papers in a graduate class and do a thesis or dissertation. They provide primary data that is easily retrievable.

We are therefore at the end of the school year, and this book that we hope will be helpful in inspiring you to think in new and creative ways about one of the most rewarding and challenging careers-teaching. You can probably guess by now that we feel that as teachers we are not only building a career but also composing a life. As you move forward, please write us at: dlbrubak@uncg.edu or lrrycble@bellsouth.net. We promise a response.

Please use the following blank space to note your reactions to this essay. What ways do you have to record ideas for improving your teaching for next year? How can you improve your method(s) for doing this? [See Resources A, B, F, I and J.]

RESOURCES

We have developed a number of resources that have aided us in leading seminars on teacher renewal. (See Brubaker & Coble, 2005, 2007). These resources may be read and reacted to privately or in a group setting, such as a professional development workshop, a faculty meeting, a retreat (something we prefer to call an "advance" to convey our support for active application) or a book club.

The resources speak to and inform themes in the stories in the previous section of this book. Each resource is designed to stimulate thought and discussion followed by concrete plans for next steps in the classroom and/or school. You will discover in using the resources that there will be a variety of responses on the part of participants. It is our view that this is not only inevitable but desirable, for there is no one right answer for most of the challenges facing teachers. Furthermore, teachers may well change their answers to such challenges in different seasons of their careers. (See Brubaker & Coble, 2007, Chapter 7.)

RESOURCE A

A CLASSROOM CONSERVATION AND CHANGE INVENTORY

What are three things in my classroom that I highly value and want to conserve?

1. _____

_____

2. _____

_____

3. _____

_____

What are three things in my classroom that I want to change?

1. _____

_____

2. _____

_____

3. _____

_____

RESOURCE B

A SCHOOL CONSERVATION AND CHANGE INVENTORY

What are three things in my school that I highly value and want to conserve?

1. _____

_____

2. _____

_____

3. _____

_____

What are three things in my school that I want to change?

1. _____

_____

2. _____

_____

3. _____

_____

RESOURCE C

QUESTIONS IMPORTANT TO TEACHER LEADERS

The following questions may be useful guides as you are engaged in professional decision-making:

1. In whose interest is this decision? [Who profits?]

2. Whose ox is gored? [Who suffers?]

3. How shall we live together in the classroom? In the school?
   [The constitutional issue.]

4. How shall I live with myself? [The personal issue.]

5. How is critique helpful in this situation? [*Critique* is summary, adoption
   of a point of view, and gathering support for this point of view.]

6. What is the transactional context, the complex mix of relationships among
   persons within a setting, and how does it influence my decision-making?

7. What is the core of my work, the centerpiece that holds everything together?
   [If I enjoy the core of my work, I feel good about my work and myself.]

8. Who defines the core of my work? [What is the degree of influence
   and the kind of influence each person has on me and my work?]

9. How can I work creatively in bureaucratic structures that are inevitable in
   schools and schooling?

RESOURCE D

ENTRANCE AND EXIT RITUALS FOR STUDENTS

What entrance rituals for students *presently* exist in your school?

1. _____

2. _____

3. _____

What entrance rituals for students *should* exist in your school?

1. _____

2. _____

3. _____

What exit rituals for students *presently* exist in your school?

1. _____

2. _____

3. _____

What exit rituals for students *should* exist in your school?

1. _____

2. _____

3. _____

RESOURCE E

ENTRANCE AND EXIT RITUALS FOR PARENTS

What entrance rituals for parents *presently* exist in your school?

1. _____

2. _____

3. _____

What entrance rituals for parents *should* exist in your school?

1. _____

2. _____

3. _____

What exit rituals for parents *presently* exist in your school?

1. _____

2. _____

3. _____

What exit rituals for parents *should* exist in your school?

1. _____

2. _____

3. _____

RESOURCE F

WORKING ALONE AND WORKING WITH A TEAM

A school based on democratic tenets recognizes and values autonomy (working alone) and working as part of a team. It is a challenge to each leader to find the most satisfying balance between these two ways of operating.

We have found the following exercise helpful in that it promotes honest communication as to how each person has fashioned a professional life that includes working alone and working with others on a team.

Please complete the following paragraphs:

1. There are times when I enjoy working alone. Some of these times are…

_____

_____

2. Some of the reasons why I enjoy working alone are…

_____

_____

3. There are times when I don't enjoy working alone. Instead, I want to be with others as part of a team. Some of these times are…

_____

_____

4. Some of the reasons why I enjoy working on a team are…

_____

_____

How do you know when you are a team member? Please make a check mark in front of the items you support.

1. I recognize that what I do affects others on the team as well as those the team influences.

2. No one on the team projects the feeling that he or she is better than others.

3. I am privately willing to acknowledge other team members' talents and contributions.

4. I rarely feel lonely.

5. I rarely feel down but instead feel lifted up by other team members and those I influence.

6. I feel energized.

7. I discover human and nonhuman resources I didn't know I had.

8. I have the courage to do what is right.

9. My vision for the future is sharpened, thus motivating myself and others.

10. I can agree and disagree with team members without taking this personally.

11. I can try out or practice new ideas and skills while having a safety net of team members to support me.

12. I am encouraged to take risks that I otherwise would be reluctant to take.

13. Principals and/or central office leaders encourage and reward me for being a team member.

14. Members of the team celebrate my victories.

15. Members of the team may well become my friends as well as my professional colleagues.

RESOURCE G

WHAT WORKS AND DOESN'T WORK IN DOING PROFESSIONAL DEVELOPMENT?

You may do this exercise alone or in a small group. If you are in a small group setting, name (a) a facilitator and (b) note taker or reporter.

Please identify and place in priority order three things you've discovered do work well in doing professional development and three things that don't work well in doing professional development. (Priority order refers to strength of response.)

Three Things That Work Well in Doing Professional Development:

1. _____

2. _____

3. _____

Three Things That Don't Work Well in Doing Professional Development:

1. _____

2. _____

3. _____

If you have met in a small group, have each group's note-taker or reporter summarize findings from small group deliberations.

_____

_____

_____

_____

_____

_____

_____

_____

_____

_____

RESOURCE H

TURNING BREAKDOWNS (LOSSES) INTO BREAKTHROUGHS (VICTORIES)

Pat Conroy(2002), author of *My Losing Season*, the story of his senior year on The Citadel's basketball team, gives us sound advice on what we can learn from losses: "Losing prepares you for the heartbreak, setback, and tragedy that you will encounter in the world more than winning ever can. By licking your wounds you learn how to avoid getting wounded the next time." He adds that he believes this "because you have to face things clearly and you cannot turn away from what is true" (p. 395).

Please list some of the losses you have experienced. Follow each loss you have identified with the lesson you learned from this experience.

Loss	*Lesson Learned*
_____	_____
_____	_____
_____	_____
_____	_____
_____	_____
_____	_____
_____	_____

RESOURCE I

MINIMAL CRITERIA FOR
PROCEEDING WITH A REFORM EFFORT

Seymour B. Sarason (2002), Professor Emeritus of Psychology at Yale University, poses a series of questions central to your teacher leadership as you participate in reform efforts.

Sarason introduces his key questions with an overall question: *"What are the minimal criteria by which you will decide whether to proceed with a reform effort, or, so to speak, forget it?"* He adds, "enthusiasm, a high level of motivation, a laudable desire to rectify or improve an unsatisfactory state of affairs, a vision of what can and should be-these, like love, are not enough, hence the astronomical divorce rate and dispiriting reform failures" (p. 113).

Sarason's key questions follow (pp. 113-114):

1. *"What is distinctively different about the setting in which you seek to effect a change?* For example, what are the formal and informal power arrangements? What happened in the past in this setting when changes were effected? What is the setting's history with regard to turnover of personnel?

2. *"Do you have criteria and ways to determine the degree to which those who are the objects of change see a need for change?* Ideally, the gravity system of the target to be changed see such a need for change. However, in most situations there are degrees of resistance to change on the part of those who are targeted.

3. *"Have you built into the change process meetings or forums in which you and the participants review and assess what has happened or has been accomplished or not?* To have such review and assessment mechanisms allows for mid-course corrections.For internal and external consultants to build in these mechanisms makes the consultants more credible and shouldn't threaten the consultants' future employment in the school and/or school system.

4. *Because you know, you certainly should know, that one source of failure of a reform effort is that a person in a key role-such as the principal or superintendent-has decided to leave, what agreement should you seek that gives you a role in selecting a replacement?* If you have a say in who should be hired to replace an existing principal or superintendent, you will feel ownership and responsibility for the success of this leader. A sense of team leadership is essential for continuity of any reform effort.

5. *Given the above questions, and assuming that you have dealt with them conceptually and realistically, do you have the funding, personnel, and time to do justice to the implications of these questions?* Anyone who has been involved in reform efforts knows that there are no quick fixes and there are always more needs and desires for additional human and non-human resources than anticipated.

Note: Please delete, revise and/or add to this list of questions based on your experience with reform efforts.

RESOURCE J

THE POWER OF CRITIQUE

Critique is the lifeblood of teacher decision-making. It is sometimes defined as the art or practice of criticism. Critique can be much more than this deficit definition that focuses on what is wrong or missing, however. Critique occurs when the teacher leader (a) reviews what has taken place, and (b) adopts a point of view (thesis) as to what took place, and (c) supports this point of view or thesis. Please give examples of your engagement in critique during a typical workday:

1. _____

2. _____

3. _____

What are some of the subtle dynamics involved in bringing excellence to critique? The first is *discernment*. To discern is to see clearly or differentiate the important from the less important. Making such a judgment always depends on a particular *context,* the situation in which the decision is made. In other words, one must move beyond generalizations to describe clearly the particulars of what is happening within a context.

Please briefly describe a difficult situation in which you used discernment within a particular context to reach what you considered to be a fair and reasonable decision.

_____

_____

_____

RESOURCES

Albright, M. (2006). *The Mighty and the Almighty*. New York: HarperCollins.

Armstrong, K. (2004). *The Spiral Staircase*. New York: Anchor Books.

Auerbach, R. & Feinstein, J. (2004). *Let Me Tell You a Story: A Lifetime in the Game.* New York: Little, Brown & Co.,

Brubaker, D. (2006). *The Charismatic Leader: The Presentation of Self and the Creation of Educational Settings.* Thousand Oaks, CA: Corwin Press.

Brubaker, D. & Coble, L. (2005). *The Hidden Leader: Leadership Lessons on the Potential Within.* Thousand Oaks, CA: Corwin Press.

Brubaker, D. & Coble, L. (2007). *Staying on Track: An Educational Leader's Guide to Preventing Derailment and Ensuring Personal and Organizational Success.* Thousand Oaks, CA: Corwin Press.

Buckley, W., Jr. (1970). *Airborne.* Boston: Little, Brown & Co.

Califano, J.A., Jr. (2004). *Inside: A Public and Private Life*. New York: Public Affairs.

Callahan, S. (1986). *Adrift.* New York: Ballantine Books.

Conroy, P. (2002). *My Losing Season.* Garden City, NJ: Doubleday.

Darling-Hammond, L. (2007, January 10). A Marshall Plan for Teaching: What it Will Take to Leave No Child Behind. *Education Week*, pp. 48 & 28.

Dreyfuss, R. (1986, March 23). Interview. *Parade Magazine*, pp. 6-7.

Ehrenreich, B. (2005). *Bait and Switch.* New York: Metropolitan Books.

Friedman, T. (2005). *The World is Flat: A Brief History of the Twenty-First Century.*
New York: Farrar, Straus and Giroux.

Friedrich, O. (1991, January 28). Yo-Yo Ma's Crazy Adventure. *Time*, p. 99.

Gibran, K. (1923). *The Prophet.* New York: Knopf.

Gladwell, M. (2002). *The Tipping Point: How Little Things Can Make a Big Difference.*
New York: Little, Brown.

Graham, K. (1997). *Personal History.* New York: Vintage Books.

Johnson, M.C. (2006, November 30). Neighbor Reaching Out With Simple Greetings.
Greensboro News and Record, p. B1.

Kidder, T. (2009). *Home Town.* New York: Washington Square Press.

Kidder, T. (2003). *Mountains Beyond Mountains: The Quest of Dr. Paul Farmer, a Man
Who Would Cure the World.* New York: Random House.

Kimball, C. (2002). *When Religion Becomes Evil.* San Francisco: Harper.

Krauthammer, C. (2005, April 9). Farewell to a Fine Magazine.
Greensboro News & Record, A9.

Livsey, R.C. & Palmer, P. (1999). *The Courage to Teach: A Guide for Reflection and
Renewal.* San Francisco: Jossey-Bass.

MacNeil, R. (2003). *Looking for My Country: Finding Myself in America.*
New York: Doubleday.

McCormack, M. H. (1984). *What They Don't Teach You at Harvard Business School.*
New York: Bantam Books.

McCourt, F. (2005). *Teacher Man.* New York: Scribner.

Mitchell, A. (2005). *Talking Back.* New York: Viking.

Palmer, P. (2002). Afterward: What I heard them say. In S. Intrator (Ed.), *The Courage to Teach: Honoring the Teacher's Heart* (pp. 309-318). San Francisco:; Jossey-Bass.

Palmer, P. (1999). Appendix A. The clearness committee: A communal approach to discernment. In R.C. Livsey in collaboration with P. Palmer. *The Courage to Teach: A Guide for Reflection and Renewal.* San Francisco: Jossey-Bass.

Palmer, P. (2002). Foreword. In S. Intrator (Ed.), *The Courage to Teach: Honoring the Teacher's Heart.* (pp. xvii-xviv). San Francisco: Jossey-Bass.

Peck, M.S. (1987). *The Different Drum.* New York: Simon & Schuster.

Peck, M.S. (1978). *The Road Less Traveled.* New York: Simon & Schuster.

Petrilli, M.J. (July 26, 2006). What works vs. Whatever works: Inside the No Child Left Behind Law's internal contradictions. *Education Week*, pp. 36 & 44

Rooney, A. (July 9, 1987). No Laughing Matter. *Greensboro News & Record*, p. A13.

Sarason, S.B. (2002). *Educational Reform: A Self-Scrutinizing Memoir.* San Francisco: Jossey-Bass.

Schlesinger, A.M., Jr. (2000). *A Life in the Twentieth Century: Innocent Beginnings*, 1917-1950. Boston: Houghton Mifflin.

Steinem, G. (1992). *Revolution from Within: A Book of Self-Esteem.* Boston: Little, Brown.

Vaughn, R. (November 30, 2006). This Fan Has Made Part the Center of Her Attention. *Greensboro News & Record*, pp. B1 & 3.

Sachs, A. (2006, November). Rock Survivor. *Time*, p. F10.

Toffler, A. & H.(2006). *Revolutionary Wealth.* New York: Knopf.

Welsh, P. (1987). *Tales Out of School.* New York: Penguin.

Yankoski, M. (2005). *Under the Overpass.* Sisters, Oregon: Multnomah.

ORDER FORM

You can order *Teacher Renewal: Stories of Inspiration to Balance Your Life* by calling School Leadership Services at (336) 712-3396, Monday through Friday, 8:00 a.m. through 5:00 p.m., eastern standard time. Orders may also be placed by mail or fax. If possible, please furnish a street address for shipping purposes. Your order will be sent by DHL or US Mail.

Payment may be made by personal check or money order.

Resource	Price	Qty	Total
Teacher Renewal: Stories of Inspiration to Balance Your Life	$19.95	_____	$ _____
Please Note: Shipping and Handling Fee: $4.95 per book.		**Sales Tax 7% (NC Only)**	
The Shipping and Handling cost is for one item shipped within the continental US by US mail or DHL ground service. If two or more items are ordered, the shipping cost will be adjusted, based on the total weight.		**Shipping and Handling**	
Overnight delivery is available for an additional cost. Quantity discounts are also available.		**Total Cost of Order**	

ON TRACK PRESS, INC. • PO BOX 157 • CLEMMONS, NC 27012
PHONE: (336) 712-3396 • www.schoolleadershipservices.com